Dedicated to my three daughters

Hafsa Alisha and Summer Jacqueline Lewis

Chapter 1

Peering out of the Victorian sash window, and looking over the rose arch that Grandad had built in the garden at Manor Farm, I saw Daddy in the distance putting our six geese away in their pen for the night. I sat at my desk and started to write a poem about my holidays and dancing on Hayling Island Beach with Nanna Lewis in front of her bright sunshine yellow beach hut. I never did do very well at school, and loved staring out of the classroom window towards the dance studio to see what was going on. "If only Jacqueline would concentrate more in class, she could have achieved so much more," my annual school report would always say. I loved to dance, but at thirteen years old and fourteen and a half stone and not having attended a dance class since I was three, all the odds of a career in dance were against me.

Luckily for me, the boarding school in Sussex, St Annes, that I had begged my parents to send me to, had closed after my first term there, and the only school that would accept me during the academic year was Hurst Lodge School in Sunningdale owned by Doris Stainer, sister of the famous actor Leslie Howard and friends with Dame Ninette De Valois and Anna Pavlova. It was a small school with small classes and lots of elderly teachers. At Hurst Lodge school, we had two houses, De Valois and Howard. On my first day at school I was put into Howard, oh, how I longed to be in De Valois. As I was escorted to my new classroom by the headmistress, Mrs Merrick, in my grey skirt, pretty blouse and school pinny, which we always had to wear. Miss Stainer believed we should learn to dress like ladies so we were allowed to choose our own blouses to wear to school. Mrs Merrick opened the classroom door and the class stood up and curtsied. It was a school tradition that whenever a teacher came through the door we had to stand back, hold the door open and curtsey. Mrs Merrick then ushered to my new desk and I sat down next to another new girl. Her name was Vicky Smit. Little did I know that we would remain very good friends till this day.

The next day I had my very first ballet class with Mrs Brooker who trained with Marie Rambert at the Rambert School. I was much taller than all the other girls in my class, and not knowing any of the steps, I was sent immediately to the back line. My heart sank as being overweight, I looked dreadful in my leotard and tights, and did not know which way to turn.

The following term, Mrs Brooker had left and we had a new ballet teacher, Mrs Brown. She was awful, and to get out of her classes, I would deliberately forget my ballet kit. Mrs Brown was very strict and cruel, and made me stand on a chair in the corner of the dance studio in my knickers and vest as a punishment. We nicknamed her "The Brown Cow". Fortunately, Mrs Brown left, and a new ballet teacher arrived in her little white Mini. Her name was Gillian Dunn, and that is when my career in dance began. I loved Mrs Dunn's classes, as not only had she been a professional dancer with Ballet

Rambert, but a wonderful teacher who believed in me and inspired me to achieve my very best.

Each year at school, a list of candidates would be put up on the school notice board outside the dance studio, and we would all run to the dance studio to see if our names were on the list. And there it was, in black and white, my name on the list. "Jacqueline Lewis - Grade 2 Cecchetti Ballet." I could not wait to get home to tell my family that I was going to take my first ballet exam, I just had to pass. From that day onwards, my school life changed forever. No more staring out of the classroom window; maths lessons became extra ballet lessons and my mind was made up. If Mrs Dunn's dance classes could make me feel so good, I was also going to become a ballet teacher when I finished school, and teach children to dance and feel special too.

The results came in, my heart pounded as I ran as fast as I could towards the dance studio. There it was, on the notice board, once again in black and white, "Jacqueline Lewis has passed her grade 2 ballet exam". Although I had only achieved a pass, I felt like a famous ballerina. But this feeling was not going to last long, as little did I know, my home life was going to change forever.

Around a week after I received my results, I was playing with my younger siblings Vanessa, Suzanne and Nigel, when my Mummy came in and sat us all on Vanessa's bed. She said, "Daddy and I are no longer going to live together". I felt a dagger going through my heart, as this was a huge shock. Mummy and Daddy had never argued, and we were brought up in a loving, happy, safe home. I was old enough to realise that this would change my life forever, and it sure did. I asked my parents if I could become a weekly boarder at Hurst Lodge, as I wanted to be as far away from the situation as possible. The following week, I had moved up to Grade 3, and Mrs Dunn asked me if I would like to assist her with the younger children on Saturday morning. I was so excited, what an honour to be asked to help Mrs Dunn.

It was perfect timing as I was feeling heart-broken with not much to turn to at the time. So now I would be able to stay over at school on Friday night, and help Mrs Dunn on Saturday morning, causing me to cast my mind away from the struggles going on at home and focus on making my dreams a reality. Saturday morning came and I woke up. I was in Peach dormitory, on the top floor. Above my head was a very large poster of Donny Osmond with his lovely smile and brilliant white teeth. I jumped out of bed with joy, put on my dance clothes and ran downstairs to the dance studio.

As I opened the blue door and walked into the studio surrounded by mirrors and barres, sitting on the chair in front of the window was Mrs Dunn and Cathy with her bottle of Coca-Cola was sitting at the piano. It was not really Coca-Cola, as I would find out many years later, but whisky. Despite this, she was a brilliant pianist and loved playing all kinds of music, especially jazz. Her husband Gordon was also a pianist, and he played for us during the week. I walked over to Mrs Dunn. She sat there looking as beautiful as ever with her hair in a bun and when she saw me, she jumped up and introduced me to Vanessa Gardner, who had successfully auditioned for The London College of Dance and Drama. Although Vanessa was in the year above me at school, we remain very good friends till this day. I was so excited and honoured to be helping Mrs Dunn for my first Saturday morning at Hurst Lodge. The changing room door opened and the children skipped into the dance studio, dressed in white satin tunics with white satin knickers and pale pink ballet shoes. Mrs Dunn put the children in their lines and the class began.

Suddenly, Mrs Dunn turned towards me," Jacqueline, could you go and teach the children in the backline a pas de chat?" My heart fluttered. Could I do it, yes I could. I ran to the backline and started to teach the children their very first pas de chat. It was amazing to see the results. I broke the step down; first of all I taught them how to do a turned out demi plie followed by two high retires, and then I added a little spring, and lastly we learnt the arms, fourth on avant, with a beautifully turned head. The children were so excited and I was so pleased to see them doing so well. Time flew, and before I knew it was time for the reverence.

The class had ended, and as I was leaving the dance studio, I was stopped by Cathy in the corridor. "Would you like a lift to the station," she asked?" Yes, please." I jumped into her pale blue Triumph Herald and I was suddenly overwhelmed by a strong smell of whisky. I then realised what was in that Coca-Cola bottle. She started the engine. It was too late to get out. She drove to Sunningdale station, the little car wobbling to and fro across the road. She slammed on the brakes, the car coming to an immediate halt. I was so relieved to be on firm ground once more. She drove off, and sitting on the platform waiting for the train, I vowed to myself that, although she was an extremely talented pianist, I would never set foot in her car again.

The following year, my parents divorce was finalised, and through my grief, I found myself comfort-eating and raiding the fridge at night, just to get through the next day. My mummy was an exceptionally good cook and made the most delicious puddings, one of my favourites was her ginormous lemon meringue pie with a huge wedge of homemade meringue on top and her strawberry trifle with lashings of whipped clotted cream. I gained weight at an alarming rate, and all my clothes had to be made for me by my Nanna Willis, who was a very talented seamstress and very close to my heart. I loved her very much, but the clothes I wore made me feel different to all those around me. The girls in my class could easily go around in the latest fashions, but I had to wear shapeless, plain and dated dresses. I even had the same problem with shoes, so they had to be made for me. This, along with a lack of confidence, bullying and the other pressures of being a teenager, made me channel my efforts into the only positive thing in my life; my dancing.

I worked really hard in my ballet classes and I was entered for my Grade 3 Cecchetti. However, my sadness and weight caused huge difficulties for me and the examiner, Margaret Valentine, failed me. I was beside myself and I cried for a week. Mrs Dunn encouraged me to go on a diet and lose weight, as this was probably a factor of the mark Ms Valentine gave me. I took her advice, and mummy supported me by taking me to Weight Watchers once a week and I lost three stones. I retook the exam two terms later, and the examiner, Gillian Dawson, gave me Commended. Afterwards, I realised it is not until you fail an exam that you actually realise how hard it is to pass.

It was my last year at school, and time for my careers interview with the headmistress, Mrs Merrick. I stood outside of her office, thinking about what I was going to say and then the door opened. "Come in, Jacqueline", she said. She was dressed in a tweed suit, and had short cropped black hair. She sat at the desk with her legs crossed, swinging backwards and forwards, and asked me what I had decided I would like to do when I finished school that year. "I would like to be a dance teacher."
"Oh dear, that is not a proper job. I think you would make a very good nurse. You are very good at looking after people."
"Oh no, Mrs Merrick, I have spoken to Mrs Dunn and she agrees that I should audition for dance colleges this year." Mrs Merrick looked astonished, and then she very swiftly showed me out of her office. There was no way I was going to be a nurse, my mind was made up.
After I finished helping Mrs Dunn on Saturday morning, and due to my dreadful experience riding in Cathy's car, I decided that I would do the three mile walk to Ascot High Street to meet my daddy in his butcher shop, after he had finished work. On one occasion, it was a very warm day and when I arrived, Daddy was still scrubbing the blocks and closing up the shop. I asked him if he could drive me to the local ballet shop in Wokingham, which he did, as I wanted to buy my first copy of the Dancing Times. Having heard about the Dancing Times at school, but never owning my own copy, I was very excited. As we entered the shop, Daddy slumped in the chair as he was exhausted, from having worked so hard that week at his butcher shop. I remember before work Daddy would wake up at five o'clock in the morning, to go to market to buy his meat before he opened his

butcher shop. As Daddy sat in the chair, I tried on some new dancewear that I needed for school and put it on the shop counter along with a new issue of that month's Dancing Times. Daddy pulled out a wodge of ten pound notes from his trouser pocket,"I hope I am not wasting my money buying this magazine," which was 40p at the time. I said ,"No Daddy, you are not wasting your money. Anything you buy for me to do with dancing will benefit me in the future ." I promise.

When I got home, I could not wait to run up to my bedroom and read my new Dancing Times. As I turned the pages, I saw many adverts for dance colleges, having made up my mind that I was going to be ballet teacher and having just passed my Grade 3 ballet exam I decided to apply for every one. The minimum entry was Elementary, at that time I believed that I was really good at ballet and no one would ever find out that I had not passed my Elementary. Once again, the odds were against me.

I remember it well; it was during the school holidays and the letters came through the post. I opened them very carefully, my first audition was for the Royal Ballet School in London. I was so excited, but how was I going to get in? I had only passed my Grade 3 and I had never been to London in my life. On my audition form, I had written that I had passed my Elementary Cecchetti in order to have my application accepted. Mummy and Daddy said that they would take me for my first audition. We took the train to London and my Nanna Willis had warned me to, "Be careful, as there are lots of pickpockets in London and they might steal your watch or purse on the escalator."

I was focused and ready for my audition. I told myself I just had to get in. We arrived at Waterloo. It was very busy, noisy and there were people everywhere. My parents decided to take a taxi, since they had never been to London before. We took a black cab to the Royal Ballet School on Talgarth Road .

I walked through the door into the magnificent building and we were ushered into a changing room. I could see the other girls and boys warming up, they were all so good. I felt butterflies in my stomach, just watching them point their toes made my feet look like flippers. We were called into the dance studio, and one by one, were told where to stand at the barre. The music began; the exercises were really hard but I tried my very best. We came into the centre, and did a beautiful port de bras, followed by an adage, pirouette and grande allegro. At the end of the class, we had to put on our pointe shoes, the adjudicators watching us as we all tied our ribbons. I had done very little pointe work and found it really hard to get right up on pointe. They wanted us to do pose turns from the corner, one at a time. I was absolutely terrified, and when it was my turn, I had no choice but to go for it. I hobbled across the room, on a bent leg trying desperately not to come off pointe, but I knew by the looks on the adjudicators faces that I had not got in, as they turned and whispered to each other.

My next audition was for the Arts Educational in Tring. My sister, Suzanne had already started Arts Educational in London from the age of 11, she was an excellent dancer in ballet, modern and tap, gaining honours in all of her exams. The day of the audition came, and we got into the car and started the long journey to Tring. As we drove up the driveway, in front of me was the stunning 17th century mansion house. As I entered the building, I loved the atmosphere of the school and I kept thinking of Julie Andrews in The Sound of Music. As this was the school she went to before she became famous. Just maybe I could become famous too. Not only did I have to dance at my audition, I also had to act and sing. Fortunately I had passed all my Lamda and Guildhall Speech and Drama Exams up to Grade 8, and I loved to sing. My trembling hand held on tight to the brass handle on the studio door. The bell rang, it was my turn, as I entered the studio, with its high ceilings and ornate decor, Mrs Jack, the principal of the school, was sitting on the audition panel and asked me to perform my song first. I sang "Out of My Dreams" by Oscar Hammerstein II and Richard Rogers and as the music started to play, Mrs Jack sat up, her eyes popping out of her glasses. She was overwhelmed by my singing voice, and commented on how wonderful it was. She said that I should pursue a career in musical theatre, and not ballet. As I left the building to get into the car, I felt my audition had been very successful.

The following week, the audition results came through and unfortunately because of my weak dancing, I was not accepted at The Arts Educational. I decided then I would go onto my next audition, at The London Studio Centre. Once again, we jumped on the train to London. As I arrived at the College, the atmosphere was very different to my previous auditions. The studio was a large hall with portable ballet barres and looked very poor. I remember it well; Donald McAlpine was taking the class. I had never been taught by a man before and this was my very first experience of a male ballet teacher. His class was difficult and fast-paced, with lots of complicated enchainments and pirouettes.

Madame Bridget Espinosa was the owner of the school and Doris Barry who was the sister of the famous ballerina Alicia Markova was her assistant. We did a full class, and then one by one, we were called into Madame Espinosa's office for an interview. Suddenly my name was called and I was shown to her office. Madame Espinosa was sitting at her desk with her little dog in a basket next to her and Doris Barry sat on another chair. I was blown away as they began to speak to me. She said, "Jacqueline, you have lovely long legs and a beautiful singing voice. You should definitely pursue a career in musical theatre." I said, "Oh no, I really want to be a ballet teacher." "Well," she said, "What I would like you to do is to go to Bellairs in Guildford and study there for one year until you gain your Elementary Cecchetti ballet exam. If you are successful, I would like to offer you a place at my school in London. Now, I am coming down to teach at Bellairs next Wednesday and I would like you to come to my classes, and we will see where we can go from there."

I rushed out of the building. I could not wait to tell my parents what Madame Espinosa had said.

I was accepted at Bellairs, a twenty minute drive away from my home, and this is where I was going to spend the next year, making sure that I achieved my Elementary Cecchetti Ballet exam at the end of it.

Hurst Lodge School, Sunningdale

Ballet Classes at Hurst Lodge

Chapter 2

It was the end of the school year and we were all preparing for our school open day, which was always held on the beautiful grounds at the back of Hurst Lodge School. I had choreographed a dance called "The Toy Shop" and included my sister Suzanne, who was going to be the ballerina. Wendy, who lived around the corner from Nanna Willis in Sandway Road, had made Suzanne a beautiful pale pink tutu. Suzanne's friend Jill was going to be the rag doll and Selina was going to be the Jack in the box, I also had a gollywog and a clown in my Toy shop dance. In my dance classes I had learnt a modern, tap and ballet dance, and in my drama class I had prepared a speech from Shakespear's "A Midsummer's Nights Dream ". I was going to be the character Oberon. I loved open day. As well as inviting all our family and friends to watch us perform on the lawn, there was also prize-giving followed by a scrumptious cream tea.

After we finished performing all our dances and speeches, the headmistress Mrs Merrick would stand behind the table full of beautiful shiny trophies and lots of shields, glimmering in the sunshine. It was a real honour if you received an award as you could have your name and the year engraved on the trophy. As we all sat quietly in lines on the grass, Mrs Merrick called my name. I was thrilled, my last year at school and I had won the Progress Cup for Ballet and the Choreographic Award for my Toy shop dance. I loved the years I spent at Hurst Lodge School, it was more than just a school, it was a big family.

I was in the bottom group for French with Mademoiselle Helsby, a short middle aged lady, who wore thick dark rimmed glasses and a wig on her head called Fred. In the green cupboard by her desk she kept a jar of sugar almonds and every French lesson we would play Lotto, although I did not learn any French grammar , I very quickly learnt my numbers in french, I wonder why? I remember one maths lesson at the end of the Summer term, when Juilet Smith padlocked Mrs Hampshire's handbag to the chair and took the key to the padlock on holiday with her to Malaysia and when the night before we left school we wrapped toilet paper around all the pine trees in the school grounds and the following morning at our very last school assembly, as we sang "God Be With You Till We Meet Again", all you could see out of the studio window was hundreds of toilet rolls, hug like streamers from pine tree to pine tree across the school grounds. Mrs Merrick, the headmistress was so appalled, that she made us spend the whole afternoon having to remove them. Then there was the night, when I was a boarder at school and we decided to raid the school tuck shop. My best friend Mandy, who was the smallest and the lightest girl in the class, slipped through the bars in the tuckshop window and passed out packets of Walker's salt and vinegar crisps and a variety of Cadbury's chocolate bars, what a magnificent midnight feast we all had that night. As the school building was very old and every floorboard creaked, we all thought the school was haunted. One cold, dark, windy night we had a seance in our school dormitory and we believed that we had brought Miss Stainer back from the dead! We sat crossed legged in a circle with a turned over glass in the middle, we had cut out letters from the alphabet and spread them out around the glass. As we turned off the dormitory lights everything went pitch black, the curtains were swaying back and forwards in the howling wind that was blowing through the cracks in the Victorian sash windows. Then to our horror the glass began to move and we all screamed as it moved faster and faster, pushing the letters out around it to spell MISS STAINER, it was true Miss Stainer was still walking the floorboards at Hurst Lodge School. That summer I left school and I was so excited to be going to the Cecchetti summer school at Lilleshall in Shropshire, as I had never been before. My friend Silke had very kindly offered to give me a lift in her boyfriend's car. Once we arrived, we were shown to our dormitories. I was sharing a dormitory with Teresa Ferguson. I was only 16 and Teresa was older than me and she had been to Cecchetti Summer Schools before. The following morning, I went to my first class, and in those days, all the "hierarchy", as we called them, would sit on chairs or benches, and watch every class. It was so intimidating, as they would whisper amongst themselves about each student in the class and make comments about us if we were not correctly dressed for class.

One morning at the end of our ballet class, I was called to one side by Gillian Dawson and Moira Kennedy, the organisers of the Cecchetti Teachers Summer School at that time "We have noticed that you have not got your Cecchetti Elementary examination. In order to come to this summer school, you have to have passed your examination." They were very abrupt and upset because they said I had lied on my application form. I was very lucky that they did not send me home.

The summer holidays flew by, it was September 1980 and I started Bellairs, now the Guildford School of Acting. I arrived for my first Cecchetti Elementary Ballet class and my teacher was Angela Hardcastle. As we progressed through the class, I worked so hard that my whole body was aching and I was perspiring from head to toe. Then we had to walk across the road to another studio for our National Class with Robert Harold. I will never forget the day when he was teaching us a national dance in his class, and Mr Harold called me "The Incredible Hulk". Although he has passed away now, I still have never forgiven him for saying that.

Wednesday came and as promised Madame Espinosa arrived at the Studio, with her little dog in his basket and taught a wonderful open ballet class, with lots of stretching. Madame Espinosa was very strict and everybody was frightened of her, but we all had great respect and always tried our very best in her classes. I enjoyed my time at Bellairs, but I was not really happy there, as it felt like there was something missing. I was going through the motions of the dance classes, only to get the Elementary Cecchetti that I needed. It was not really my kind of college because there was not enough ballet for my liking. Whilst at Bellairs, I made friends with Lia Williams, she was a very strong dancer and we enjoyed spending time together outside of college. Lia always wanted to be an actress and although we are no longer in contact with each other, Lia recently played Wallis Simpson, Duchess of Windsor in The Crown.

The end of the year came and I was entered for my Elementary Cecchetti. Fortunately, I passed, and Madame Espinosa offered me a place at the London Studio Centre. How exciting I was going to live and study in London at last. During the summer holidays I continued my subscription with the Dancing Times. I have always loved to read the Dancing Times, with its very interesting articles and stunning photographs of dancers from all genres. Suddenly, as I turned the page, I saw a new college called the London School of Classical Dance. I had to apply, as it was a Cecchetti Ballet School. Molly Lake, who was trained by Enrico Cecchetti, the method's creator, was one of the teachers at the college. Molly had also danced with Anna Pavlova in her touring company. I went for my audition and I was accepted, and the following September, I moved up to London and started my training.

It was a small college, and classes were held at 90 Hodford Road in Golders Green. During my first year there, I was taught by many professional dancers, the majority of them had danced with the Festival Ballet and the Royal Ballet Company in London. Anita Young, John Travis, Belinda Wright, Jelko Yuresha, Laura Wilson, Juan Sanchez, Len Martin, John Raven, Belinda Quirey, Nicole Ribet and many more professional dancers who at the end of their dance career had become teachers. I stayed in lodgings in Golders Green with Natasha Lisakova and Zbyshek Lisak, who were the owners of the college. They had two young daughters Tamara and Nadya, who were both excellent dancers. As Tamara was a termly boarder at The Arts Educational School, Tring, I would stay in her bedroom whilst she was away at school.

Around a year after I had joined the college, Molly Lake and Travis Kemp, Molly's husband, had decided to leave the school and set up their own school in St. John's Wood. I then had to decide whether I was going to stay at the London School of Classical Dance, which later became the West Street School in Covent Garden, or join the Lake school of dance in St Johns wood. After a great deal of thought, and knowing that Cecchetti Ballet was my passion, I followed my gut instinct and I decided to train with Molly Lake and Travis Kemp. I learnt so much from Molly, who had studied with Astafieva and Cecchetti. Molly had danced in the companies of Pavlova and Markova-Dolin. In 1945 she co-founded the EmbassyBallet (subsequently Continental Ballet) with her husband , Travis Kemp, and M.Honer, In 1954 she was appointed director of the Ankara Conservatoire and remained there for twenty years, returning to London to teach at the London School of Contemporary Dance and at her own school which I joined in 1981. Molly was well into her eighties when she began teaching me and she was a true inspiration. I can remember that every morning, she would come into class and warm up with us. Her leg would go well over her head and Travis would assist her by walking around the class, correcting us.When I am teaching my classes today I can still hear Molly shouting at me, get into the ground, bend your body, touch the floor. use your space, do not dance on top of the floor. One day Molly and Travis invited all the students to their beautiful home in St John's Wood, to show us their Sydney films on their home projector presenting exclusive ballets that Molly had danced in with Anna Pavlova and also footage of Travis when he danced with Molly in the Markova-Dolin Ballet. For my birthday Molly gave me an Alabaster egg, which I still have sitting in my glass cabinet today. Molly said that she wanted to give it to me because I was always smiling in her classes. Looking back over my dancing years, I was so fortunate to have met and been taught by all these wonderful teachers. At that time I just thought it was normal, now later on in life, I realise how fortunate I was to have had these very special people in my life.

While at Molly's school, where there were no more than twenty of us, Once a week Eve Pettinger would come and teach us associate classes. Eve was a wonderful teacher so clear and thorough. I remember once at a Cecchetti Summer School Eve asked me to be her guinea pig, in a mock associate exam that she was going to examine, in front of all the students, teachers and examiners at Summer school. I felt so honoured to be asked to be Eve's guinea pig and In 1985 I gained my Cecchetti associate with Diana Barker and Margaret Marsh as my examiners. Molly and Travis found me my first teaching job, teaching young children to dance at Cresswell Hall, in Kentish Town, London.

I taught at Cresswood Hall in Kentish Town for many years, commuting every Tuesday from Woking station, after I had finished my part time sales assistant job at Next. The caretaker of the hall was a lovely lady called Bobbie, she was an authoritative figure and excellent at dealing with all the parents. This allowed me to concentrate on my teaching and the welfare of all my students. One of my very first students was Ihsan, who was seven years old when she joined my classes. Ihsan was very keen to learn and always wanted to work hard in class, trying her very best to get everything correct. Then came Lauren, Sarah, Aliya and Ben, who all went onto successfully audition for the Junior Associate Classes at The Royal Ballet School in Talgarth road. They were all very fortunate to have been taught by Jocelyn Mather, who previously had also taught at Hurst Lodge school in Sunningdale. Although the journey to Cresswood Hall was far from where I lived, I really loved teaching my students. They all came to ballet because they wanted to learn, very different from today, where ballet is mostly treated like an after school club. Our first examiner was Eileen Langman, who trained with Mary Skeaping, Margaret Crask. Helen Wolska and Laura Wilson . Having recently passed my associate Cecchetti, Eileen was my very first examiner at Cresswood Hall and what an inspiration she was. After our first successful exam session, I invited Ursula Hageli and Richard Slaughter from Ballet Creations of London, to do a workshop for my students. I had met Ursula and Richard at Molly and Travis's ballet classes at The Lake School in St John's Wood. It was a wonderful workshop and a huge success, most importantly all the students thoroughly enjoyed it.

After graduating from college, I set up my own Dance School in Byfleet Village Hall, which I named The Lewis Academy of Dancing. I continued to commute to London once a week as well as directing and teaching at The Lewis Academy of Dancing, both dance schools worked alongside each other, gaining excellent exam results, and many of my students that I had taught went on to professional training and careers in dance and teaching. On Sunday 3rd June 1990 I was awarded the Peter Pearson scholarship to attend the Cecchetti Summer School. The Peter Pearson scholarship came out of the associate group which Cara Drower organised for 13 years, until it became the Cecchetti Teachers Association, organised by Tessa Barker, and after Alison Dos Santos and Diana Cremona. It eventually folded in 2004, when Cecchetti teachers showed no interest in the new qualifications, DDI and DDE.

After I had finished teaching, every Saturday afternoon I would take the train to London and attend the Intermediate and Advanced Cecchetti classes at the Cecchetti Centre at Dance Works in Balderton Street, which in 1992, moved to the West Street School in Covent Garden and then to London Studio Centre from 1993-2012.

It was at 90 Hodford Road, on Saturday 24th September 1983 where I met Richard Glasstone, who was to teach me for my Licentiate and Fellowship Cecchetti, and became an important figure in my dancing career.

The Cecchetti Centre was founded by Richard Glasstone with proceeds of the gala performance he organised as a tribute to his teacher, Nora Roche. The gala was held at Sadlers Wells Theatre in London on the 16th January 1983. Richard officially opened the Cecchetti Centre which I attended, on Saturday 24th September at 90 Hodford Road, Golders Green, in the presence of guest of honour, Dame Ninette De Valois. Dame Monica Mason, Dame Antoinette Sibley and Lesley Collier OBE who all became patrons of the Cecchetti Centre. Diana Barker was chairman of the Cecchetti society at the time and Barbara Fewster was the Ballet Principal at the royal ballet school. There were many other guests, but these were the VIP's.

As well as attending the Cecchetti Centre, I also really enjoyed attending the Cecchetti Friends lectures, which were first held at the Gentlemens Club, and then, due to high attendance, were moved to the University Women's Club. The Cecchetti Friends ran for two years, with a lecture a term. Monica Mason gave the first lecture. The lectures were given by many experienced and highly esteemed individuals, such as Barbara Fewster, Beryl Grey, Deborah Macmillan, Bryony Brind, Fiona Chadwick, Ross Alley and Richard Glasstone. I enjoyed these meetings, as not only could you listen to their valuable knowledge, but you could talk to the individuals, and ask questions.

After leaving The Royal Ballet School, Richard became Director of Ballet at Laine Theatre Arts in Epsom, not too far from where I lived in Byfleet, Richard coached me for my Licentiate Cecchetti exam and invited me to Laine Theatre Arts to teach the students under his watchful eye.

It was a wet, windy morning and Grandad Willis drove me to Laine Theatre Arts. As I got out of the car, the heavens opened and I was drenched from head to toe. I ran to the front door of the school where Richard was waiting for me. As I approached him, he said, "Would you like to go into the changing room to dry off?" I was so nervous, I said, "Oh no, don't worry, I will be ready to teach the class now." I went into the studio, dripping wet, and put on my ballet shoes. Richard turned towards me and said, "I am so sorry Jacqueline, but we have not got a pianist today. You are going to have to sing to the students while you teach them." I could not believe it. The students walked in, beautifully dressed, and my class began.

At the end of the class, after the students had left, Richard sat me down and pulled my class apart. I felt devastated, as the exercises I had prepared were just not good enough. Richard set me some homework for the following week, and asked me to rearrange my exercises to teach to the students again. As I left the school, it had stopped raining, and grandad drove me home.

As the weeks progressed, and my teaching improved, I had organised my class for my Cecchetti Licentiate examination, and decided to enter myself for my exam. The following week I told Richard what I had done. He was alarmed, "Jacqueline you are nowhere near ready to take your exam." It was too late as I had paid my exam fee to the ISTD and I could not get a refund. I worked so hard, I just had to pass my Licentiate. I could not let Richard down.

It was the day of my Cecchetti Licentiate examination, and I took the train to London. I arrived at the ISTD headquarters and went through to the changing room to get dressed. I walked into the studio. My examiners were Victoria Chappell and Eileen Langman, and they were sitting behind a large table. I had also been allocated students from various colleges around London to be my pupils for my examination. I started my class, which was going very well and then out of the blue, Mrs Chappell asked, "Can we stop for a minute?" I thought, what have I done wrong? "Do you mind if we open the window?" Phew! I thought to myself. "Yes, of course, please do."

I carried on my class, the students trying their very best to help me through my examination, by working hard and listening to all my corrections. Then we came into the centre and I had to teach the first set of port de bras as well as various adages and enchainments from the Intermediate syllabus. . My class finished, and Mrs Chappell asked me if I had any questions.

"Yes, when can I have my result, please?"

Both examiners glared at me through their glasses. "You do not ask questions like that."

"But the foreign students who take their examinations always get their results straight away." Eileen Langman looked at me, "If you would like to go and wait outside dear, we will see what we can do."As I sat in the changing room, I could not believe what I had asked, and I convinced myself that I had failed my exam. As the door opened, Elieen Langman stood in the doorway, holding a small piece of white paper which she handed to me and then she promptly left. As I opened the paper with trembling fingers, I could not believe my eyes. I had passed my Cecchetti Licentiate examination with Distinction! I could not wait to tell Richard.

I put on my long royal blue coat with my matching blue Wellington boots that came just above my ankles and I ran as fast as I could to the tube station. I arrived at Dance Works in Bolton Street, where Richard was teaching his class at the Cecchetti centre. I threw open the studio door and ran inside the studio. The students were Darcey Bussell, Viviana Durante and Tetsuya Kumakawa along with many of my dancing friends, including Lisa Rager, Deborah Smith and Rachel Hester. They were all shocked to see me enter the ballet class in my wellington boots at such speed. The class came to a halt and I ran up to Richard who was standing at the piano. "Richard, I have passed my Licentiate exam. I have gained a Distinction!" Richard gave me a big hug and congratulated me. It was the happiest day of my life.

At 16, attending the London School of Classical Dance.

My students at Cresswood Hall, Kentish Town

Chapter 3

After gaining my Licentiate Cecchetti with distinction, I continued teaching at my own dance school, The Lewis Academy of Dancing, at Byfleet Village Hall and attended Advanced classes at The Cecchetti Centre with Richard on Saturday afternoon. During the week I went to Advanced Cecchetti classes with Gillian Dawson at Lyne Village Hall. I went on to purchase Gaynor Morton's school, as she was retiring. She had two branches in Elstead and Guildford. At this time I was still teaching in London. I was also working part time at Next in Woking five days a week, in order to earn enough money to be able to save for a deposit for my first mortgage. At that time, I was living with my grandparents in Byfleet and one morning, as I had just finished my breakfast, I opened the local newspaper, The Informer, to see that they were selling studio flats in Byfleet village, I thought how lovely it would be to have my own home, so I enquired about getting my first mortgage with Jackie Jarrett at the Alliance and Leicester in Woking. In order for me to buy my first home for the sum of £52,500, I had to prove that I was earning enough. I had saved my ten thousand pound deposit, being self-employed it was very difficult to get a mortgage, so my daddy very kindly offered to be my guarantor. This enabled me to get my first mortgage and purchase my first studio flat in Wakefield Close Byfleet.

My new home was just around the corner from Byfleet Village Hall. It was lovely to have my own space so close to my dance school. My new neighbour Steve Finch, a piano teacher at Guildford Grammar School, very kindly offered to play the piano for my School Show at The Queen Elizabeth School Woking. I had written a song for the finale which was called "A Bit of a Do at the QE2," and Steve composed the music for the song. I organised a coach to bring my students down from my school in Kentish Town, London to Woking, so both my schools could take part in the performance together. The show was very successful and everyone enjoyed themselves, my school grew from strength to strength, pupils continued to gain excellent results in their Cecchetti ballet exams and successfully auditioned for colleges, going on to perform around the world. After passing my Licentiate Cecchetti I went on to take my Advanced Cecchetti gaining a Merit, I then decided I would start to study for my Cecchetti fellowship. I continued my classes with Richard at the Cecchetti Centre on Saturday afternoons and encouraged three of my senior students Raquel Gavira, Rhian Emanuel and Nicole Miller to join me. Raquel, Rhian and Nicole were all Cecchetti Scholars, along with my former pupils Kate Hatefield and Becky Honey.
The Cecchetti Centre had now moved from Dance Works into the premises of The London Studio Centre, King's Cross. Richard suggested that I could prepare my class for my fellowship exam working each week with my three advanced students. I will forever be grateful to Richard as after we had finished dancing in the Intermediate and Advanced syllabus classes, Richard would stay on at the centre and help me free of charge to prepare my class with my

three students for my fellowship exam. For my exam I also had to write an essay and I decided to write about my connection with Molly Lake and her connection with Enrico Cecchetti. Richard once again very kindly offered to correct and help me with my essay. To enable him to do this, once I had finished my essay, I would post it to Richard and he would correct it and post it back to me.

The following week I said to Richard " I do not think I am ready to take my fellowship this term," Richard said, "Jacqueline you are ready!"

As I have always loved a challenge, I decided that myself and my three students would all take our exams on the same day at the ISTD headquarters in London. Rhian and Nicole took their Intermediate Cecchetti, gaining honours. Raquel took her Advanced Cecchetti also gaining honours and I took my Fellowship, which I successfully passed. Since that day I am so proud to be able to write the letters FISTD after my name.

After gaining my Fellowship in the Summer of 1999, I felt it was time for a change. I applied for a teaching job at the Marion Lane School of Ballet in Cyprus, Marion Lane telephoned me to ask if I could teach for her the following term. Unfortunately I was unable to find a Cecchetti ballet teacher at such short notice for my school in Byfleet, therefore I could not accept her offer. I did not want to be an elderly lady sitting in my dance studio with a cat on my lap, having never explored the world and as I had always fancied being a holiday rep, I decided to rent out my house, find a Cecchetti ballet teacher and one cold November evening in 2001 I decided I would complete the application forms and apply to become a holiday rep with First

Choice holidays. I was offered an interview which was successful and I was sent to attend a training course in Cyprus the following spring, which I thoroughly enjoyed. I was offered the position of a sovereign representative in Cyprus ,my dream was always to work in Corfu. I decided to take a £200 a month drop in salary Which at that time would leave me with £400 a month. I was offered a position as a mainline representative on the beautiful island of Corfu in Greece, little did I know that this would be the beginning of a new chapter in my Life.

No one could understand having just passed my Fellowship, why I would want to leave my school in the good hands of a fellow teacher and travel to Greece, to be a holiday rep for £400 a month. My nanna Willis was shocked along with my other dance colleagues and teachers.

I knew what I was doing and having never gone to university I needed to travel and experience another side to life. I had been to Corfu on holiday with my good friend Julie the previous Summer and fallen in love with the beautiful Island.

That April I packed my bags and flew out to Corfu. At the airport I was met by the manager Claire from First Choice holidays ,who drove me to my apartment in Kontokali ,where I was going to spend the next six months, living and working with a team of people I had never met in my life.

I can honestly say becoming a holiday rep was one of the most challenging things I had ever done in my life. I had only travelled abroad once as a young child and, unable to speak a word of Greek I had definitely thrown myself into the deep end, with no lifeguard to save me. Having never worked in a team and always been my own boss, this was my first challenge. As well as sharing an apartment with two other reps half my age, working day and night in forty degrees of heat, covered in mosquito bites from head to toe and guests shouting at me due to their room not having a sea view. I remember one day finishing my shift at the airport at 5 am. as there had been a delay on the flight coming in and then having to travel to the far north of the island, around the numerous hair pin bends up and down narrow mountain roads to deliver my guests to their Apartments and hotels.

Walking on narrow dirt tracks through dark badly lit fields, full of humming and clicking giant beetles and bugs, holding my torch thumbling in key safes trying to find keys to open up apartment doors and showing my guests into their apartments. Guests tried and confused after their long travels and trying to find their way in the dark, moaning and groaning as they went. Afterwards there was no time to sleep, I had to go straight to my welcome meeting to meet my new guests who had just arrived on their holidays. I worked six days a week from 8 a.m. until 8 p.m., and two nights a week I also had Airport duty . On my day off I would just collapse, too tired to do anything. Partly because most nights of the week I would be partying the night away. One week I was so poorly with sickness and diarrhoea, my manager told me to go to the doctors and have an injection to stop it, as she could not afford me to take a day off work. I felt I was in the Army, a world away from the life at my Dance School.

At the height of that Summer I had had enough and decided it was time to look after myself, rather than please my manager. I was completely exhausted and had to think of a plan to make my life easier, to enable me to complete my very long first season with First Choice. It was my turn to do another night shift at Corfu Airport. I had seen my guests onto their plane and I was just about to do my welcome speech to my new guests that had just arrived in Corfu. When I had an idea! What if I could ask them to check in with the hotel receptionist at their varios hotels, then I could go back to my apartment and get some sleep. Thinking that was a very reasonable idea I included it in my welcome spiel on the coach before we left the airport and told all my guests that I would meet them the following morning, at my welcome meeting in the hotel lounge just next to the hotel reception area. Unfortunately my plan did not go as expected and the coach driver told my manager what I had done. The following day I was called into her office and given a written warning. Were my days in Corfu numbered? Should I take another chance?

I had met two young men from England at Gouvia Marina and they had offered to take me out on their boat for the day and show me the amazing coves and beaches that could only be reached by boat. I really wanted to go and decided it was time for plan B. That evening I put a sign on my hotel notice boards, to let my guests know that I would be doing a training course with First Choice and I would not be on duty the next day. I was so excited about my first adventure on a private boat, my friends Jan and Louise came too. Rob and Colin sailed their boat out into the clear turquoise blue Ionian sea, as we all sat on deck looking back over our shoulders leaving Corfu Town behind us. As we sailed out to sea Rob suddenly turned off the engine of his boat, ahead he had seen a school of dolphins. With great excitement we all dived off the boat into the darkest blue sea I had ever swam in, then suddenly I thought, what would I do if a dolphin swam up next to me and what if I saw a shark, I then remembered, when I was a child I had watched Jaws 2 at the cinema with my 3-D glasses. Was my vivid imagination getting the better of me.

Rob and Colin then sailed into a tiny cove, they anchored their boat and we all swam ashore and had a delicious barbeque that they had prepared for us. What a magical training day it was, one I will never forget for the rest of my life and no one ever found out! For my first season I was given a car, a royal blue Renault twingo. I had never driven a car abroad before, let alone on the other side of the road. I was petrified having to drive up and down mountains, around hairpin bends, with no road lights or lines in the middle of the road. The wonderful thing was I felt free, nobody knew me, nobody judged me and everyone liked me for the person I was. I felt like a tonne of bricks had been lifted off my head, this was a new beginning, wonderful friendships were made and I felt so attractive. Gone were the days where I had been overweight and had felt I was just not good enough at anything I tried to do. For the first couple of months I felt so guilty, that I had abandoned all the students at my dance schools. I would dream that I was teaching them in a multi-storey car park, as they held onto the concrete pillars for their ballet barres.

My first summer season in Corfu was coming to an end, what a wonderful summer it had been. On the last night of the season we had a team jolly and what a great evening it was. We all met at Miltos Bar in Kontokali. Miltos was an excellent Greek dancer, and very handsome, with a wonderful personality. Miltos would always teach us and encourage us to join him in his Greek dances. I loved to dance with Miltos, he would set fire to the floor in his bar and we would dance in front of the flames, dancing the Sirtaki, Ikariotikos, Kalamatianos, Hasapiko, Tsamiko, Pentozali and the Sousta. That night as we left Miltos bar, there was the first storm of the season and what a storm it was thunder, lightning and an extremely heavy downpour of torrential rain. The road outside the bar was completely flooded and had turned into a river. My friends and I had brought new lilos that day, luckily we had them with us. I had an idea to jump on our lilos and float back to our apartment, together, so at 2am in the morning that is exactly what we did and what fun we had, getting completely soaked from head to toes we laughed all the way home, our lilos completely destroyed after our journey.

Early Thirties, as a Holiday Rep for Tui in Corfu.

End of Season party with First Choice

Chapter 4

I did not want to go back to England. I had seen a job advertised in the August edition of the dancing times magazine. Two sisters on the Island of Capri in Italy were looking for a Cecchetti ballet teacher to cover their maternity leave; they both owned the only dance school on the Island of Capri. I applied for the teaching job, immediately they responded to my CV and asked me if I would like to teach for them. I explained that I had to finish my contract with First Choice holidays until the end of October and then I would fly out to Italy.
I flew to Naples and took the boat to Capri. When I arrived I was met by both sisters who showed me to my very small studio apartment and then invited me to their home to have dinner. The next day they took me to their dance studio which was underneath a beautiful 5-star hotel next to the limoncello factory on the magnificent island of Capri. I could not speak a word of Italian and very quickly I learnt a few important words to enable me to get through my classes. As I only worked part-time at the dance school there was very little else for me to do when I was not teaching. I was extremely lonely and the following term I decided to go back to England.
It was a very difficult decision as nobody at the dance school wanted me to leave, the owners begged me to stay as they had no one else to teach for them and the parents of the students wanted to find me a husband so I could stay and teach their children forever. Apart from the very first day when the sisters had invited me to their home for dinner , there was very little interaction between us, they were both

heavily pregnant and I felt I was left alone to run the dance schools. When you live on a small Island in winter and you do not know anybody and you cannot speak the language, you live and eat and teach alone, gradually you start to feel quite depressed, this was a feeling I had never had before and I knew it was time for me to go back to England. I can remember Mary Jane Duckworth who was the chairman of the Cecchetti Society at that time, calling me at home and telling me how disgusted she was that I had left the sisters without a teacher. I tried to explain to her how it felt teaching alone in Capri. but she did not understand. From that day onwards, I have always felt a black mark above my head from the Cecchetti Society, which is completely unnecessary.

I was invited to go back to Corfu to do another summer season with First Choice, fortunately for me I worked in five star hotels and villas on the island and then one day I was at the First Choice office in Potamos and that is where I met Sally, who was a wedding rep for First Choice. Sally invited me for dinner at her home in her village, called Pelekas, which was on the west of Corfu. Little did I know that Pelekas would become my second home even to this day. While I was sitting on Sally's balcony watching the sunset, I fell in love with Pelekas. I asked Sally if she knew of any houses for sale in the village. Sally said it was very hard to find a house in the village, as the houses were passed down to the children in the family and very rarely sold. Nevertheless she would keep her eyes and ears open and let me know if she heard of anything for sale. Pelekas village is idyllic with the beautiful sandy beach of Kontogialos just a walk away. I love to swim in the fresh, clear turquoise waters of the Ionian sea. While I was working for First Choice and living in a rep's accomodation in Kontokali. I would always drive to Pelekas after I had finished my morning duties at my last hotel, The Corfu Palace in Corfu Town. I had a company car which was a white Fiat Seicento. I loved driving down the steep mountain to Kontogialos beach to have a swim and a spot of lunch at Spiros Taverna, before driving back to my hotel for my evening shift. One August day I had just got into the sea when I heard a distant voice coming from behind me. Hello are you Jacqueline Lewis the ballet teacher, as I turned around quickly I thought I was going mad, hearing things, echoes of guilt in my head. having deserted all my students at my dance schools in England. Hello, do you remember me? You taught my sister Ihsan at Cresswood Hall in Kentish Town many years ago, she would love to see you. With that Ihsan came running over through the hot golden sand. I could not believe it after all these years one of my very first students was standing next to me on Kontogialos Beach, was this an omen?

Little Did I Know from that day, every year Ihsan and I still meet up every Summer in Pelekas village.

About a year later Sally called me to let me know that Stathoula and Nondas Kontis were selling their house for fifteen million drachma, approximately £30,000 at the time. This was way over my budget as my life savings were £20,000, Which I had been saving since I was thirteen as we had lived on a farm. I had really wanted to buy a horse. When I realised that I was not cut out to clean the stable before school, I started saving for a sports car. I promised myself I would buy one for my 40th birthday. Once I arrived in Pelekas I decided that this would be a complete waste of money and buying a holiday home on the beautiful island of Corfu would be a better choice. The next day I met Sally in Pelekas Cafe and we walked through the village until we reached the top of the mountain. It was extremely hot and as we approached the house, Stathula was sitting outside, there were lots of cats running around the courtyard and flies buzzing above our heads. Stathula offered us a glass of lukewarm orange Fanta, which I politely sipped as we sat down outside the house.

Spatula then proceeded to show me the house, as I walked through the front door the smell of urine was overwhelming, on the floor were layers and layers of old lino, the lino had been thrown on the stone floor, one layer on top of the other, as the last layer had worn out. There was also a bathroom in the corner of the room that had been built with breeze blocks and a big rusty tank hanging over the top of the bathroom. In front of the kitchen window was an old stove, the glass pane in the window above the stove had been cut to enable the pipe to go through the window to the outside courtyard. There were also a couple of very old dark brown dingy, dirty cupboards. I stepped down a steep step from the kitchen into the bedroom and there was Nondas, Stathula's husband sitting on the bed. The bedroom was a long narrow room and at the end of it was a small window. I opened the shutters and in front of me was the most beautiful view of a valley with a high mountain in the distance. As there were no internal stairs in the house, one had to go outside to get to the first floor. In the courtyard there were metal stairs and railings leading up to a balcony on the first floor. I opened the door, there was a large bedroom with a small ensuite shower room , two large windows and four single beds.

Stathula explained to Sally, as I could not speak a word of Greek, that this room was used to accommodate tourists during the summer season. Next to the house was a small apartment. It looked like an old shop front with a very large window and an adjoining door. Years ago it must have been an apothiki or a donkey's shelter. As we entered through the metal door, a wooden wall had been erected to make two separate rooms, there was no window in the back room and it was very dark and gloomy. Stathula also rented these rooms to tourists and told us what an excellent business it was. Each morning she would go to the village square and catch the tourists as they got off the number 11 bus and drag them up the mountain with their heavy rucksacks. As they reached the top, they were too hot and bothered to leave and they would stay in Stathula's apartment before looking anywhere else.

We left the house and Sally invited me to her house to discuss our visit. I was alarmed to think Sally would show me a house that smelt of urine and was so dirty, dark and dingy. Sally said, "Jacqueline looked at the potential. It is in a nice quiet area and you will have plenty of space for your family to come and stay for the holidays." I thought about it long and hard and decided Sally was right. I was going to buy Stathula's house, but there was no way I was going to pay fifteen million drachma for it.

The next day I went back to the house and pretended that I was looking at the house opposite, Stathula came running out of her house, waving her hands in the air at me, "Down, down, down!" she shouted. By reading her body language, I think she was trying to tell me that she was going to bring the price of her house down. Not being able to speak a word of Greek, I smiled and left. Days went by and I could not stop thinking about owning my own house in Corfu. It was my day off and I decided to drive to Pelekas and go for a swim on Pelekas beach, which was at the bottom of the mountain before you entered Pelekas village. After my swim, I decided to go and visit Statula, and as I approached the top of the mountain, Georgios, Stathula's next door neighbour, got hold of my hand and pulled me into his house. He wanted me to buy his house. I then realised that everybody who lived on top of the Mountain wanted to sell me their house. Georgios's house was very small and had a cesspit under the kitchen floor for the disposal of sewage, as the house was not connected to the main drainage. The house had a small balcony with an amazing view over the whole of Corfu town. I was very tempted to buy Georgios's house because of the view, but I realised that no one would be able to come and stay. As I was coming out of Georgios house, Stathula ran up to me, held my hand and dragged me down a small alleyway (Smelly Alley) to a small cafineo in the village square, we went inside and I met Stathula's son and daughter. Alexandra, Stathula's daughter spoke pigeon English she sat me down and brought me a drink, "We want you to buy my mother and father's house, we are tired of walking up the mountain to look after them both and now it is the time for both my mother and father to come and live with us in our house in Vatos."

"I only have ten million drachma, if you want me to buy your mother's house, this is my highest offer." Immediately Alexandra accepted my offer and in the background Stathula was shouting "Eleven million! Eleven million!" Alexandra said, "No, Jacqueline can buy the house for ten million drachma", so now I had to find a lawyer. It was a very hot Monday morning , as I drove into Corfu town and managed to park the car close to the Corfu Palace Hotel. I strolled around the town visiting many lawyers on my way and then I arrived at Mario Papetis's office. As I climbed the steep marble stairs to the third floor, I turned the corner and there was Mario's office. I knocked on the door, an elderly lady with dyed jet black hair opened the door and showed me in. "Please wait here for Mr Mario". A few moments later Mario popped his head around the door and ushered me into his office. Mario sat down behind a grand desk, the walls behind him were covered in certificates he had achieved at law college. On his desk were ornate paperweights and stunning photo frames with photos of his family inside.

Mario spoke to me in fluent English and immediately I knew this was the lawyer I would choose for the purchase of my house in Pelekas. "Mario please can I ask for your advice, I have seen a small village house in Pelekas I would like to buy for ten million drachma", and I proceeded to show Mario the papers.

"Jacqueline this is the price of a car in England, you cannot make any mistakes if you purchase this house." I left Mario's office and on my way back to my car I took a walk along the Liston, one of the most central and famous places in Corfu. The pedestrian street of the Liston, is located at the end of Spianada, the main square of the Island and the largest in the Balkans and is also the main entrance to the famous narrow cantons of Corfu Old Town. Next to it, there is a large area with grass where cricket matches and other events take place from time to time. It has been said that Liston means on the list, at Libro d'Oro that is, where the names of nobles and aristocrats of Corfu Were written, and who only had the right to enjoy their walk on the pedestrian street. As I made my way along the famous Liston I felt honoured and happy to be in Corfu and now I was going to buy and own my own property there too.

I remember it well, the day I bought my house in Pelekas. I met Statula and Notis at the notary office in Corfu Town and they had insisted they wanted me to buy their house in cash rather than do a bank transfer. I had my money transferred from England into my Greek bank account and luckily at the time there was a good exchange rate from pounds into drachma. I will never forget it. On the day of the sale I queued in Alpha bank on san roca square for nearly an hour. There was no air conditioning in those days and it was stiflingly hot inside the bank. The cashier then gave me a bag of cash, ten million drachma to be exact. As I left the bank carrying this ginormous bag of money, for the first time in my life I could imagine how a bank robber would feel, looking around me as I went as fast as I possibly could in the extreme heat of Corfu town until I arrived at the notary office of Phillis Papetis. I sat down on a chair that was outside his office clutching my bag of money waiting to be called in, there was no turning back now. The door opened and as I walked it the first thing I saw was Stathula's big smile, as I approached her with the ginormous bag of ten million drachma, I handed it to her thinking that she would then hand me the keys to my new house, well very old house in the mediaeval village of Pelekas. I was astounded and astonished that Stathula tipped the bag of money onto Phillis's desk and started to count it. I thought to myself we are going to be here all night, as she dropped some notes on the marble floor and started to count the drachma from the beginning again! Phillis Papetis explained to me that Stathula wanted me to go to her house to collect the keys. I left Corfu town and drove back to Pelekas, leaving my car in the square. I climbed up the mountain once more to my new, but very old stone house. Stathula was sitting outside amongst all her cats sipping her glass of orange fanta and then in her broken English and my broken Greek we managed to communicate with each other. Even though the house now belonged to me, Stathula was not at all ready to move out and she asked me if she could stay until the following month. I had no furniture in Corfu and really did not think that Stathula would want to carry all her old furniture down the mountain. I suggested that in return for her to stay in my house for another month, she could leave all her furniture behind for me. Stathula agreed and the following month she moved out and I moved in. I never gave it a thought what her fellow villagers would think of an English woman buying her house and living in their village.

Stathula eventually moved out of her house in Pelekas and I finished my first Summer season with First Choice. Watching the last flights leave from Corfu Airport , I was looking forward to spending my first Winter in my new home in Pelekas. I finished work at the end of october, the weather was still warm enough to go to Pelekas beach and swim in the sea. It was idyllic as there were no tourists left on the Island, no sunbeds and umbrellas smothering the golden soft sand leading to the crystal clear turquoise water. I swam alone in the calm sea, hundreds of fish swimming underneath me, as I turned over onto my back and looked up the mountain towards Pelekas Village I realised I had not just bought a home but a slice of paradise as well. As the winter nights drew in, Pelekas became very quiet and I felt very isolated living alone in my house. I had no internal staircase and to get to my bathroom I had to go outside and use the cast iron spiral staircase, leading up to my balcony and bedroom door. I had no problem doing that in the Summer, but in the Winter it was a different story! During the Winter in Corfu it would rain for a week, triancial rain, without stopping. Even with an umbrella it was a challenge just to go upstairs to the bathroom, let alone going to the toilet in the middle of the night. The humidity was so bad, that when I woke up in the morning to put my clothes on, they were soaking wet. My first winter in Corfu was survival, completely opposite to the summer. Thank goodness, that summer I had met lots of new friends and one very good friend till this day is Wendy. I met Wendy just after I had moved into my new but very old house in Pelekas. I was shopping in Delias, the Italian supermarket in Kontokali buying buckets and brooms and Wendy was behind me at the till also buying buckets and brooms. I turned around and joked with Wendy about us being very Greek, as all women in Corfu own their own buckets and brooms. Wendy and I are still the best of friends to this day. Nan Wen, as my three daughter's call her, has become a very important member of our family and we still both love cleaning our houses with our buckets and brooms from Delias, the Italian supermarket in Corfu today. One afternoon I was sitting on my small hard wooden settee in my salon, when there was a loud cracking noise around me, suddenly my salon roof completely fell in, just missing my head, I was so lucky I did not get hurt, but not so lucky that I had to pay to have a whole new roof put on my house, all the joists were completely rotted and the roof had just caved in around me. Another time I was watching Greek television on my small portable TV and that night there was a huge storm with electric lightning, a thunderbolt shot through my salon window and hit the TV, which blew up in front of my very eyes. After that winter I decided that I would not spend another winter in Corfu.

Mario is my lawyer to this day and he was right. Twenty years later I am still happily enjoying living in my village house in Pelekas with my three daughters Shannon, Hafsa and Summer during the summer and Easter holidays. We all love our holidays in Corfu and feel a huge sense of belonging. Over the last twenty years the villagers of Pelekas have become our very good friends. The girls say, mummy when we come to Pelekas, it feels like we are part of a very special family.

As my first Winter in Corfu was coming to an end it was time to return to my job as a holiday rep with First Choice. One morning I was on duty at Kontokali Bay Hotel when I was approached by Carol, a manager from Tui, who offered me a job as an a la carte representative, it was an offer I could not refuse. I would be working in the best hotels in Corfu, have a company car and Tui would also give me a monthly living allowance on top of my six hundred pounds a month salary, as I would be living in my house in Pelekas. I continued working for Tui for the next couple of years, my dance schools in England were still open, although student numbers had dropped, since I had stopped teaching at the schools.

While working for Tui, I really missed my dancing and decided that I would start my own dance company in Corfu. I called my company Corfu City Dancers. Having worked at the best hotels in Corfu, I now had very good connections with the hotel managers and also realised that there was not enough entertainment for my guests in the evening at their hotels. I came up with a brilliant idea: one of my students in England, Raquel Gavira, was coming to the end of her three-year professional training course at Central Ballet School in London. The timing was perfect, as Raquel and her friends Hannah, Sarah and Samantha were preparing to audition for dance companies around the world. I contacted them and asked them if they would like to spend their summer holidays in Corfu. I also asked my friend Vanessa Gardener to see if her daughter Natasha would like to join me in my project of setting up my very own Dance Company. They all thought it was a wonderful idea and I decided that I would trial my project for one month and see if I could gain enough contracts with the hotels to audition professional dancers for the following summer. The Dancers paid for their own flights and I offered them free accommodation. The Mayor of Pelekas was very kind and offered me the use of the Village Hall in return for a free performance for the village that summer. It was a very hot August and I had driven my little white Fiat to collect the five dancers from Corfu Airport. Their names were Raquel Gaviria and Sarah Luscombe from the Central School of Ballet, Hannah Windows from the English National Ballet School, Natasha Jervis and Samantha Kettle from Rambert. The five girls were very excited to be in Corfu, they all squashed into my little car and with their luggage packed neatly in the boot and hanging out the windows. We set off for the mountainous drive to Pelekas. We arrived, I parked my car in the village square and we continued up the mountain on foot, as they all dragged their suitcases behind them. I had turned the apartment next to my house into a dormitory where all the dancers could live and sleep together. We all sat down and had a cold drink and then I showed the dancers where we would be taking our daily ballet class and rehearsing together.

The next morning we woke up early. I did an hour's ballet class with the dancers and then we began our rehearsals. I had two weeks to choreograph and rehearse the show until we did our live performances at the Imperial Hotel, the Louis hotel and the Elea beach Hotel, not forgetting the performance I had promised the village in Pelekas. I decided that I would let the dancers each choreograph their own dance for the show. I thought this would be a good experience for them, a chance to work together and to get to know each other. Natasha loved Spanish dancing and choreographed a Spanish dance to Roxanne, Raquel, Samantha and Sarah decided to choreograph a contemporary piece and Hannah choreographed a classical ballet dance on pointe. I decided that our first show would be based on Classical, Contemporary, Jazz, Tap and Spanish solo's, duet's, trio's and group dances, so that the dancers would have time to get changed in between each dance. I spoke to the hotel managers and they agreed that the dancers could have a free evening meal, when they performed at the hotel. My next step was to find costumes, not an easy task on the island of Corfu. I had asked the girls to bring with them all of their leotards, as I had decided that I would create the costumes based on what they had brought. I went into Corfu town and managed to find many nice clothes in the Chinese shop as they were very reasonably priced and an excellent addition to complete the costumes. The show was finished and we were invited by the Mayor of Pelekas to put on our very first performance at the open air theatre in the village.

The Auditorium was packed, as the whole Village had turned up for our very first performance. That evening's program consisted of The Corfu City Dancers, Laodamas folklore school in Corfu town and the ladies from the Pelekas Cultural Society. It was a hot sticky evening in the middle of August and the dancers were as hot as hell, their costumes sticking to them with the heat as they danced. I was so proud of them, they all danced so beautifully and little did I know that the Corfu Television Station was on air filming the performance. Mr. Kontis, the founder of the Laodamas folklore school, approached me after the performance, "Jacqueline, we would love you to come and teach us in the winter at our school in Corfu town." What a wonderful opportunity this would be, I could start teaching my Cecchetti ballet classes again in Corfu. October came and my season at Tui was coming to an end. I had arranged an appointment with Mr Kontis and I went into Corfu town to visit his school. The meeting went very well and he agreed that he would advertise my ballet classes for me and I could start teaching for him the following week. I was so excited; Even though I did not enjoy my last Winter in Corfu, I convinced myself that this winter would be a good opportunity for me to teach Cecchetti ballet again and I stayed that winter in Corfu and taught my new students at Laodamas. Corfu Town is the capital of the Greek island of Corfu, in the Ionian Sea. It is one of the most charming and romantic places in Greece, known for its cobblestone streets and pastel-coloured Venetian architecture. Surrounded by the sea, the old town of Kerkyra is closed between the two ancient fortresses. That winter after I had finished teaching at Laodamas, I wandered aimlessly through the narrow cobbled streets of the beautiful old Town of Corfu , a UNESCO World Heritage Site. As I looked up at the clusters of Venetian colourful buildings hovering above me. I had fallen in love with Corfu town and dreamt of one day owning my own apartment there. I remember a saying I heard very often as a child, if you don't ask, you don't get. If my father ever saw a house or a shop he liked, without fail he would always knock on the door and ask the owner if they would be interested in selling it. If there was no answer he would write a note and pop it through their letterbox. I guess I learnt the majority of my business skills through my father. The following morning I did not wake up to the sound of church bells, but to the sound of my telephone. I jumped out of bed knocking over my bedside lamp, half asleep, as I ran as quickly as I could into the kitchen to answer the telephone. It was McCarthy Stone, developers for retirement properties asking if they could buy my house in England. Alarmed and shocked, I told them that my house was not for sale, but they did not give and looking back I am glad they did not. After numerous telephone calls from McCarthy Stone, in the end they asked me to name my price. As I was not at all interested in selling my house, just to get rid of them, I asked them for four times my properties current market value and when they agreed I just had to say yes. Not knowing what to do with the money from the sale of my house in England. As I was very happy and enjoying my simple life in Corfu and wanted for nothing, I put my money in the bank and in those days I was earning twenty thousand pounds a year in interest. Having fallen in love with Corfu, luckily I had managed to detach myself from Darcey Cottage in Oyster Lane. I then decided that I was going to buy a small piece of history and that year I bought my apartment in Corfu Town. Having spent many months wandering through the cobbled streets of Corfu Town, dreaming about owning my own apartment. One day I had just finished having my iced chocolate in The Liston, when I came across a small antique shop in one of the many small streets leading from The Liston and suddenly I remembered what my father had taught me. I opened the shop door and walked inside and there sitting behind a small wooden desk on an old rickety chair was a elderly lady called Freda. Little did I know that this lady was going to take me somewhere that I had never been before. Just like Stathula had done, Freda held my hand and led me through the narrow back streets of Corfu Town until we arrived in a wonderful place next to the sea, Mouragia. I followed Freda into the grand venetian building until we reached the fourth floor and there we met Mr Spyros, who at nearly ninety years old took a very large key out of his trouser pocket and opened the apartment door. Freda and I followed Mr Spyros into the apartment and I could not believe my eyes, as I looked through the very large venetian windows all I could see was the sea, every room in the apartment had the most amazing seaview. Although the apartment was very old and falling apart I did not worry about that, I was buying a slice of history with a wonderful seaview on top.

My Students in Capri

My Village House in Pelekas

Stathula and Notis Kontis

Dancing with Miltos in Kontokali

Chapter 5

Spring was on its way and it was time for me to return to my job with Tui. It was also going to be my first six month summer season with my dance company Corfu City Dancers. I had put an advert in The Stage and any dancers who wished to apply for my company had sent me their CV's and showreels. During the winter I had chosen my four dancers for the summer season Natalie, Rosie, Tina and Becky. I could not wait to meet them in person and start rehearsing for our show. As well as the use of the hall in Pelekas, Mr Kontis also agreed that we could use his dance studio in Corfu town. I have now been offered contracts with the Imperial Hotel, Louis Grand Glyfada, Louis Keryra Golf and Elea Beach Hotel. The dancers would do a ballet class and rehearse in the mornings, have a siesta in the afternoon and perform in the evening. The dancers all worked very hard and had a wonderful summer in Corfu, an experience they will all remember for the rest of their lives.

At the end of that summer, I left Tui and decided I would focus on my dance company Corfu City Dancers, which successfully continued for the next five years. Then a recession hit Greece and some of the hotels stopped paying us for our shows. It was time for me to go back to teach Cecchetti ballet in England. My schools in England had now dissolved as I had been working in Corfu for six years. I had only intended to go to Corfu for six months. As I was reading my Dancing Times magazine, I suddenly came across an advert for a ballet teacher required to teach RAD ballet at a co-educational public school in Cranleigh, Surrey, The school was called Cranleigh School. Although it was an RAD teacher the school had advertised for, I was sure I could convince them that the Cecchetti method would be a brilliant alternative.

I called Cranleigh School from Corfu and asked to speak to the head of dance. Little did I know that when the head of dance answered the telephone it would only be my ex student Kate Hatfield. I had taught Kate from the age of seven to sixteen. Kate had successfully auditioned for the Cecchetti Scholars and at sixteen went on to train at the London Studio Centre and then went on to perform professionally on cruise ships around the world with the singer Jane Macdonald. Kate was so surprised to hear from me.

"Jacqueline, I definitely want you to come and teach me at Cranleigh School. I will check with the headmaster tomorrow to see if he is happy for you to teach Cecchetti, instead of RAD." The following morning Kate called me to let me know that I had got the job at Cranleigh School and I could teach the Cecchetti Method. Leaving Corfu was a very difficult decision, as I had made so many new friends over the last six years, I had brought my house in the village of Pelekas, started my own dance company, taught Cecchetti at Ladamas in Corfu town and not only had I fallen in love with Corfu, but Alexios Arvanitis from Pelekas too. That evening I told Alex that I had been offered a teaching job in England at Cranleigh School. Immediately, Alex said, "You must go to England and if you like teaching at Cranleigh School, stay in England and I will come to England to stay with you and find a job." While I was working in Corfu, my dearly beloved Nanna Willis passed away. During the winter months if I returned to England, I would always stay with Nanna Wills at 141 Church Road. On my return to England in 2009, I stayed with my father and stepmother in Winkfield, Berkshire, until I eventually bought my own house, a Victorian cottage in Beech Hill Road, Sunningdale. It was very strange living in England again, the pace of life was so much faster than that of Corfu. I missed my friends, the bright warm sunny days, the moonlite evenings sitting on my balcony under the shooting stars and most of all I missed Alex. I was alone, living alone and eating alone. The winter was drawing in, the days were getting shorter and the nights were getting longer. I first met Alex just after I had brought my house Pelekas. Stathula had warned me when I first met her, do not fall in love with a Corfiot man. Why not? As I had fallen in love with Corfu, what was wrong with falling in love with a Corfiot man? One of the pipes in my house had burst and I had to find a plumber. I had been told that Tellis was the man for the job. I ran down the mountain as fast as I could looking to find Tellis's house, sitting outside the house was a very quiet, good looking Greek who introduced me to tellis and very kindly Tellis came up the mountain carrying his bag of tools to help me. Little did I know that the following summer I would be meeting the good looking Greek once again. It was the middle of August and my friends and I had arranged to meet each other on Pelekas beach just in front of Spiros's Taverna. I was sunbathing with my friends and I was so hot that I just felt like going for a nice cool swim. As I ran on tip toe across the baking hot sand, I jumped into the sea and started to swim. In the distance I recognised the good looking Greek who I had met in the village at Tellis's house. He stood out like a sore thumb, as he was so pale compared to his friends from the village. I swam over to him and asked him why he was so pale and he said, "I never have time to go to the beach as I work in Archeology and I need to have my siesta." I went back to my friends. As I was lying on the beach looking up at the sky I could see a huge black rain cloud coming towards us. Surely it could not rain in Corfu during August. Then I heard a loud rumble of thunder in the distance and all of a sudden the heavens opened. As I picked up my towel there was that pale good looking Greek, he asked, "Can I help you?" Before I had answered he picked up my beach bag and we ran inside Spiros's Taverna together. Then he said to me, "Please, can I buy you a cup of tea?" And that is the day I met Alexios Arvanitis.

It was my first day at Cranleigh School and I had plenty of time to get there. I had met a car salesman called Dave in Zanzibar in Pelekas and he had kindly offered to find me a car for my budget of a thousand pounds and deliver it to my house in Sunningdale. My new car was a royal blue peugeot and I prayed that it would get me to Cranleigh school and back on my first day. Luckily it did and after an hour's drive through the Surrey Hills I arrived at Cranleigh School. Kate met me at reception and escorted me to the dance studio. Little did I know that when I opened the studio door who should be sitting at the piano, the one and only Liz Hewson. I was so excited to see Kate and Liz again after so many years and could not wait to meet my new students and get started. It was wonderful to teach in a proper dance studio with a pianist, a Harlequin floor, ballet barres and mirrors. I taught girls and boys on a Monday, Tuesday and Thursday

at the Prep and Senior school. Kate taught curriculum dance in the mornings and I taught Cecchetti ballet classes in the afternoons.
I loved teaching at Cranleigh school, after many years of running my own dance schools it was a real treat just to teach and not have to do all the admin work as well. I had finished my first term at Cranleigh School and Kate and I were invited to the school Christmas Ball. I had never been to a ball before and felt honoured to be invited. What a lovely evening it was and a chance for me to be introduced to the Headmaster Michael Wilson, his wife Carolyn and the rest of the school teaching faculty. Dinner was served in the great hall with high vaulted ceilings. I felt like I was in a scene from Harry Potter. I sat down at a very long table that was laid most beautifully with linen tablecloths and silver cutlery, the centre of the table was decorated with pretty flowers and sweet smelling candles. That evening I met Faye Nutley who taught English at the Prep school. Faye started teaching at Cranleigh School when she had finished her degree at Bristol University, Faye lived in Cranleigh village. I told Faye that I had only started teaching at Cranleigh that term, as I had been living and teaching in Corfu. Faye said that she and her friend Alicia had booked to go to Corfu in the summer holiday.
It was the Christmas holidays. I was so excited as Alex was flying to England to spend Christmas with me. There were no direct flights from Corfu to England in the Winter. Alex had to fly from Corfu to Athens airport and then take the flight to Heathrow Airport. My father had offered Alex a job at his butcher shop during the Christmas holidays. Alex had never been a butcher before but he was willing to learn and help my father during his busiest time of the

year. Most evenings Alex would arrive home completely exhausted and collapse on the sofa and fall asleep. It did not turn out to be the Christmas I thought we would be spending together. After Christmas Alex had to return to Corfu as his elderly mother had had a bad fall and being the only child Alex needed to go home to look after her. We said our goodbyes and in January I returned to my teaching at Cranleigh School.

I was in the staff room and Kate asked me if I would be interested in starting a Saturday dance school at Cranleigh. I jumped at the chance and Kate took me over to the senior school sports centre and showed me the dance studio. I met Steve the sports centre manager and we discussed our ideas together and not only did he put the new Saturday dance classes on the Cranleigh school website, he also put an advert in the local newspapers. The new Saturday School started in April and It was a huge success; not only was I teaching Cecchetti ballet, I had also introduced ISTD Modern and Tap classes.

I had always wanted to have my own family. Alex already had a daughter with his previous partner Manuela, as Manuela had returned to Germany with the baby, Alex was scared to have another baby with me and unfortunately for me, I had gone through an early menopause. Alex returned to England to work for my father in the butcher shop and that Christmas Alex brought me a beautiful diamond engagement ring and we got engaged. After a lot of thought we decided that we would try to adopt and we approached Berkshire Social Service, who invited us to an Adoption information evening which was held in Bracknell. We arrived at the meeting. As we went into the meeting, my eyes met with another lady across the room. We signed in and the organisers asked us to pair up with another couple. As I turned around, the lady I had seen when I first walked through the door approached us and introduced herself and her partner. Hello she said, my name is Julie and this is my partner Aidan and asked us if we would like to pair up with them and we did, they were a lovely couple and many years later we are still very good friends. After the meeting I was sent a letter from the organisers and they recommended that we should contact PACT in Reading.

After attending a PACT introduction evening, We were offered an interview with Pact. That Easter we had planned to go to Corfu for the othordox Greek Easter. We had a wonderful time celebrating Easter with our friends in Pelekas and Corfu Town. The Easter holidays had finished and it was time to return to England. The night before we left Alex told me he wanted to stay in Corfu and return to his work in archeology. I was shocked, angry and devastated. All I could think about was becoming a mother. As I said goodbye to Alex at Corfu Airport my dreams were shattered, I cried all the way home to England. I was alone again and what was I going to do about the adoption with a pact. I arrived at Gatwick Airport and I managed to pull myself together, as my mother had always told me to do when I was upset as a child. Leaving Gatwick Airport, I made my way to the station to get the train home. As I sat on the train my phone rang, it was a social worker from pact, I felt like they knew what had happened and I felt so stupid.

"Hello Jacqueline, is Alex with you?" I held myself together, "Alex does not want to return to England and we are no longer together. I have decided that I want to adopt on my own."

"Oh well," the social worker said, in a tone that showed no surprise or empathy,"You will have to stop the adoption process for six months in order to recover from your broken relationship with Alex." I was so angry, it felt like Alex had ruined all my chances to become a mother. Looking back, I never really thought about what Alex wanted. I only ever thought about what I wanted.

Six months passed, and I was asked to attend another interview at Pact. I passed, and they invited me to attend a two-week training course at their headquarters in Reading. I arrived for the first morning and met other adopters on the course, but I was the only single adopter. All the others were couples. We sat around in a circle, and the social workers sat behind a table. We all introduced ourselves, and then the course began. They showed us a lot of Powerpoints, videos and we also did a lot of team-building exercises. I enjoyed the courses, and I learnt a lot. I was also shocked at the amount of people who attended the courses, and how difficult it is to become an approved adopter.

That Christmas I had decided that I was going to work with the homeless in London. I wanted to understand how it felt to not have anything and to have no one to care for you. I had had a privileged life and I knew the child I was going to adopt would have come from an unprivileged background, I had to know how that would feel. I applied to work with Crisis and gave up my own Christmas to help those less fortunate than myself. I was based at a Crisis Centre on the Talgarth Road, not far from the Royal Ballet School and I decided that I was going to give dance lessons to the homeless. I had an idea that if they completed my class I would give them a certificate. I had no idea how difficult it would be for them to finish the class. I was allocated a room to teach in, men and women of all ages who had never danced before would wander in and out of my dance classes. The smell was deadly, the participants had not washed or changed their clothes for weeks. I kept focused and remembered while I was there and continued to teach my class. At the end of each dance class the adults that completed the lesson would be given a certificate. It was wonderful to see their faces and how proud they were to have achieved something and be recognized for their achievement. At lunchtime I sat in the canteen having my lunch and listening to them all talking to each other about my dance classes. After lunch they would bring their friends along, as they also wanted to get a certificate.

After my training with Pact I was allocated a social worker who would visit me every week and completely interrogate me until she had completed my PAR. By the time I went to the adoption panel my social worker knew more about me than I knew about myself. After nearly 2 years of complete interrogation and numerous training courses, I was finally approved to become an adopter and then the matching process began. Although I thought after becoming an approved adopter for a child 0-4 years, I would be able to choose the child I wished to adopt. I was wrong; the social care system is engineered so that Social services decide which child you are able to adopt. In the following months I was sent profiles of various children from all over England from the ages of 0-4 years. The profile would consist of a white A4 piece of paper with a photo of the child and a short description about the child. As I looked through the profiles with great excitement and enthusiasm, I selected a couple of children that I felt drawn to and emailed my social worker to let her know. My social worker replied, "Please think very carefully about the children that you have selected, Jacqueline." Immediately I knew that these profiles had been sent to me to test my reaction, how I had read and understood them, had I benefited from all the visits from my social worker and the numerous training courses. As the months passed, I felt very despondent and deflated as I thought that there was no child in the universe for me to adopt. Being a fifty year old single mother, what were my chances of being placed with a child? I woke up early that morning as I heard the neighbour's dog barking and then there was a knock at the front door. I opened the door. "Please can you sign here," the postman said to me. I took the large brown envelope inside and opened it. I pulled out the thick booklet inside the brown envelope, it was from Doncaster social services in Yorkshire. On the front cover there was a two year old girl called Skyler that my social worker wanted me to consider adopting. I thought to myself this is not the child for me, being inquisitive I flicked through the rest of the profiles and there was Shannon. She jumped off the page at me; that was my daughter, the child I was going to adopt. Shannon was seven and and half, I had only been approved for a 0-4 year old child, what was I going to do? I had arranged that day to go for a long walk with my friend Jill and her little black dog Wally. As we walked around Sunningdale golf course, I told Jill what had happened that morning. Jill said think very carefully about the pros and cons of adopting a seven and a half year old rather than a two year old. I went home and had some lunch and started to write down my thoughts. If I could adopt Shannon I would be able to take her to the Royal Opera House in Covent Garden to watch the ballets with me, Although I knew Shannon would come with a trunk full of excess baggage from her past, hopefully she would have a health record and being an older mother, I decided this would be a sensible decision, I emailed my social worker and, bingo! She agreed and thought that Shannon and I would be perfectly matched, but that was only the beginning. The following week a meeting was arranged at my house. Kerry, Shannon's social worker and Mel Kerry's manager came down from Doncaster to Sunningdale to meet me. I opened the front door, Kerry burst into tears and said, "I have found Shannon's mummy." At the meeting was also my social worker Helena and her manager from Pact. We all sat around the dining room table, the Yorkshire social workers were casually dressed and very friendly and down to earth and the social workers from Pact were very smartly dressed and quite standoffish. It felt like I had the Labour Party from Yorkshire and the Conservative Party from Reading sitting around my dining room table. I was so excited to meet Kerry and Mel and listen to everything they had to say about Shannon. Meeting or no meeting I had fallen in love with Shannon, the minute I saw her photograph and nothing was going to stop me adopting her.

Alexios Arvanitis

Nanna and Grandad Willis

The Corfu City Dancers

The Pelekas Cultural Society

Chapter 6

That August, I was invited up to Yorkshire to meet Shannon and her foster carer, Joy. I would stay in a cottage in Yorkshire that social services had rented for me, and spend the next two weeks getting to know all about Shannon, before I brought her home to Sunningdale. I remember it well: it was a warm sunny August morning and I took the train from Sunningdale to Waterloo and then the underground to Kings Cross, from King's Cross I took the train to Doncaster. When I arrived at the station in Doncaster it felt like a different world. Mel very kindly picked me up from the station in her car and drove me to Joy's house. As we were turning the corner into the estate where Joy lived, I saw Shannon on her little yellow Dora The Explorer bicycle cycling 100 miles an hour towards Mel's car. As I jumped out of the car, Shannon threw her bicycle to the ground and ran up to me, gave me a big hug and called me Mummy. I was blown away. Joy invited us in for a cup of tea and Shannon jumped on my knee and gave me another big hug. Lacey, Joy's granddaughter and Shannon's friend who was with her at the time, was very jealous and also wanted to jump on my knee for a hug. When you are a birth mother, you make all the decisions for your child from the minute your child is born. When you adopt a child, the child you choose comes from your heart, not from your womb. Your child has lived with their birth parent or parents and foster careers from the start of their life. They have been neglected, abused and starved, they have been passed from pillar to post, like a game I used to love to play at

Birthday parties. When I was a child, the game was called pass the parcel. This time though it is definitely not a game. When the parcel lands on your lap, it is an innocent child and you have no idea what is inside, no idea what is going to come out and I can only compare the feeling to an experience I had when I was a child and so desperate to have a pet dog. My father, without thinking about the consequences, went to the RSPCA in Chobham and brought a Great Dane home. When the dog arrived we were all so excited to have a pet dog, he was taller than us all and charged around the house knocking everything down in his path. I remember it well, it was teatime and my mother had laid the kitchen table with scrumptious cream tea, we had shut the dog in the laundry room so that we could enjoy our cream tea in peace. Suddenly the dog bolted into the kitchen and demolished the entire pat of butter. The butter dish flew across the kitchen floor and shattered into tiny pieces. We all grabbed our plates of food and ran upstairs into the bathroom, locking the bathroom door behind us. We ate our tea in the bathtub that night. We had owned the dog for less than twenty four hours and my mother demanded that my father should immediately return the dog to the RSPCA. Funnily enough my younger sister Vanessa left school and became an RSPCA inspector, I guess good does come out of bad sometimes. I also had a brown and white pet Guinea Pig called Olga Da Polga, she was my pride and joy and I loved playing with her. One day my younger brother Nigel thought he would give Olga a treat and give her a bath in the garage. He found a large tub of Finish dishwasher powder and popped her in. Luckily for Olga, Nigel being only two at the time could not manage to reach the garden tap. After he had covered olga from ear to paw with white dishwasher powder, he then thought she would like to go for a run in the neighbours garden. When Nigel could no longer see Olga he ran inside shouting at the top of his voice "Uinea ig in the hedge!"

I had always wanted to learn to play the piano, we had an upright piano in our playroom at Greenways Drive which I used to make up my own tunes on. My best friend Indira and her sister Marie-Suzanne played the piano most beautifully and when I went to their house they always taught me how to play a duet with them on the piano. I asked Mummy and Daddy if I could learn how to play the piano and they thought it would be a really good idea to find a piano teacher to come to our house and teach us all. Daddy found us a piano teacher, we were all so excited and could not wait for our first lesson the following Saturday. Out of my bedroom window I could see the piano teacher coming up her drive in her bottle green car. As I was the eldest it was my turn first. Mummy opened the door and introduced us all to the piano teacher and I showed her into the playroom and sat down with her at the piano and my lesson began. While I was having my lesson, the piano teacher had left her little brown and white Jack Russell on the backseat of her car. Daddy had just arrived home from his butcher shop with a big bag of cream donuts and gave one to Nigel, while my sisters and I were having our piano lessons. Nigel clutching onto his extremely creamy donut, suddenly spotted the little Jack Russell and headed towards the bottle green car. The little dog saw Nigel and started to bark and as the little dog went berserk inside the car, Nigel ran around and around the car chasing the dog until there was no cream left on his

donut, as it was all over the car windows. The piano teacher was furious and that was my very first and very last piano lesson as she never returned. On another occasion Suzanne and Nigel decided that they were going to raise money for charity (or for them to buy sweets) and without my mother and father knowing they packed up all our toys in my Daddy's wheelbarrow and wheeled them around the estate where we lived and sold everything all our toys to the whole of Greenways Drive. My mother was furious when Mrs Lloyd called her to tell her what Suzanne and Nigel had been up to and she made them give all the money back to the residents of Greenways Drive. Once my Daddy had left his butcher's van parked on our drive and he was so tired that he had forgotten to put the handbrake on. Suzanne and Nigel jumped into the Butchers van and sat on the driver's seat, pretending to drive the van and Vanessa and I jumped in the back. We slammed the door shut and the van took off down the garden, crashing into the fence at the end of our garden where our neighbour kept her donkeys. Luckily we were all okay and the van only suffered a couple of bumps and scratches, but the donkeys had escaped and were running all over our garden.
When we first moved to Manor Farm in Binfield, the garage was full of wild cats. My mother wanted to keep them to scare away the mice, unfortunately they hissed and spat at us and scared us away instead, in the end we had to have the cats terminated, as nobody wanted them and they were too dangerous and wild to keep. When I adopted my first daughter Shannon, her behaviour reminded me of that of the wild cats at Manor Farm. Through no fault of her own, she would throw her new toys down the stairs at me, swear at me, hit me and

bite me. I can honestly say I was scared of my own daughter. Once she was asleep I would light a candle, lie in the bath and pray to god that I would get through the next day. I was frightened to ask social services for help, in case they took Shannon away from me, I loved her with all my heart. I never told my family and friends how difficult it was, they just saw a pretty little girl, they all loved having around them.

Shannon was not allowed to go to school when she first arrived in Sunningdale, although she was seven and a half years old. Pact thought it best that she stayed at home with me, until we had formed a strong enough attachment to enable Shannon to return to school. Although I was not allowed to go to work and purely for my own sanity, I continued my teaching job at Cranleigh. When I was teaching during the week Shannon would stay with my family and friends, until I got home from work. On Saturday morning Shannon would come with me to Cranleigh School. It was an hour's drive to Cranleigh and one early Saturday morning as we set off in the car together, I heard Shannon crying in the back seat. What's the matter darling, why are you crying? Mummy you have to know these are tears of pure happiness. I always wanted to learn to dance, but I never thought I would have a mummy who was a dance teacher and from that day onwards Shannon has always loved her dancing and is a beautiful dancer. I remember the very first time I took Shannon to The Royal Opera House in Covent Garden to watch the Royal Ballet's performance of La Fille Mal Gardee. I had bought two tickets for us in the amphitheatre, not knowing how Shannon would react to her first ballet performance, as she was only seven at the time. The auditorium lights went out, the audience applauded and the conductor made his entrance. The orchestra began playing the wonderful score composed by John Lanchbery and the grand red and gold heavy velvet curtains, slowly opened to reveal the Royal Ballet Company performing the choreography of one of Fredrick Ashton most joyous and colourful creations, inspired by his love of the Suffolk countryside, La Fille Mal Gardee. Fredrick Ashton is one of my favourite choreographers as he strongly supports the Cecchetti method and this can be shown throughout his choreography today. Excited and happy Shannon jumped out of her seat, luckily we were in the lower slips and there was no one sitting behind us and she remained there transfixed throughout the whole performance. I sat back in my seat, my dream had come true. My daughter loved to watch the ballet and was so well behaved. As we both enjoyed going to Covent Garden and watching the ballets, I decided that I would make this a regular event in my diary taking Shannon to see the Nutcracker, Mannon, Swan Lake, Sleeping Beauty, Romeo and Juliet, Raven Girl, La Bayadere, The Two Pigeons, Alice in Wonderland. Coppelia, Giselle, Elite Syncopations, The Judas Tree and Wolf Works.

As well as going to the theatre Shannon and I loved to travel together. We always spent the Summer and Easter holidays in Corfu, Greece staying in our home in the mediaeval village of Pelekas. In the winter we liked to go to Coral Bay in Paphos, Cyprus. One Winter I took Shannon to Tenerife and we stayed in a lovely hotel on the beach. Shannon loved the food at the hotel and thank goodness I had booked half board, as Shannon never stopped eating the whole holiday. In the restaurant it was self service and Shannon loved going to the buffet and refilling her enormous white porcelain plate. I sat at our table watching the other guests' faces, seeing this tiny skinny little girl running backwards and forwards consuming her body weight in delicious hotel food at breakfast and dinner. In October half term I took Shannon to Italy. We flew from Gatwick to Pisa and then jumped on a train from Pisa to Florence. I had booked an Airbnb in the centre of Florence. It was an old venetian building with eight floors and guess what? Our room was on the eighth floor. We shared our kitchen and bathroom with two students who were both very kind and polite. Before we had left England I had contacted Nicoletta Santoro the director of the Hamlyn Ballet School in Florence to organise for myself and Shannon to attend Cecchetti ballet classes at the school during our trip to Florence. I had also contacted Penny Whiting, a good friend and fellow Cecchetti ballet teacher who lives with her husband in Rome and my childhood best friend from Greenways Drive, Indira Graffius who lives just outside Florence. Shannon and I had a wonderful trip to Florence catching up with old friends and dancing in the magnificent studio of the Hamlyn School, I had met Brenda Hamlyn at numerous Cecchetti Summer Schools in England and although now Brenda Hamlyn had passed away, I was so excited to visit her school and see her legacy. Shannon really enjoyed her Cecchetti ballet classes with Elisa Corsini and watching me dance. One of Shannon's favourite memories of our trip to Florence was the delicious homemade lasagna that we ate every day at a very small restaurant Alessandra Alberti had shown us after one of her classes, not forgetting the amazing Italian ice-creams that we both devoured each day. What wonderful memories we have.

On our last night in Florence, Shannon and I had just finished packing our suitcases, ready for our return to England. When the chandeliers in our bedroom started swaying to and fro, the walls were moving around us. Shannon was screaming and I carried her into the Kitchen and we both crawled on our hands and knees under the kitchen table, too scared to move. The mobile phone in my pocket began to vibrate, I reached for it with my right hand, Shannon clinging on for dear life to my left arm. I answered the phone. It was Indira, "Are you and Shannon ok? We are having a huge earthquake, stay under the kitchen table and do not move."A series of major earthquakes struck Central Italy between the Marche and Umbria regions in October 2016. The quake on 30th October was the largest in Italy in 36 years, and this was the one that we experienced. We were 188.6 km away from the epicentre, and luckily for us we both survived the earthquake and were able to fly back to England the following day.

Shannon and Me on Pelekas Beach

Shannon's first iced chocolate on Pelekas beach

Shannon and me in Italy

Shannon Dancing in the Scuola di Danza Hamlyn, Florence

Chapter 7

Having come from a large family myself, I had always wanted to have more than one child and when Shannon had been with me for 3 years, I decided that I would apply to adopt a second daughter and a sister for Shannon. As I had adopted Shannon through Pact, it made sense to approach Pact for my second adoption. Unfortunately I had failed my interview, but I was not going to give up. As I was born in Woking, I decided to apply to Surrey and I was offered an interview. I arrived in Woking for my interview, which was taken by Morag, a manager from Surrey social services, unfortunately Morag was not convinced of my application and could not understand why Pact had not accepted me on their training course. I was asked to return for a second interview, where another manager was brought in to observe my interview. At last I was accepted to go onto the training course to become an approved adopter with Surrey.

My social worker was Kate and I really got on well together. After just over a year of working together , I went to the adoption panel and was approved to adopt my second daughter and a sister for Shannon. Kate had recommended that I attended an adoption day in London at Tottenham Football Club. As I arrived and walked through the door, there were social workers from all over England, standing behind tables in the large Stadium. On the tables were profiles of boys and girls and sibling groups of all ages . I decided that I would make my way around the stadium and talk to all the social workers I could, in the hope of being matched with my second

daughter. As I walked from table to table looking through lots of profiles, I came across a profile that interested me. It was that of three siblings who all had speech impairment and I thought to myself I could give these siblings a loving home and also help them with their speech. The social worker behind the table was very excited to meet me and very keen to speak to my social worker Kate about the sibling group. I made my way around a few more tables and then suddenly I came across Doncaster social services.
I was excited to tell them that I had adopted my daughter Shannon from Doncaster and that I had been approved to adopt another child. I really enjoyed the adoption day and could not wait to tell Kate all about it. The following week Kate came to the house to visit us and I told her about the sibling group. Kate said that she would speak to her manager Morag about the siblings. Unfortunately Morag's reply was, "Jacqueline, Surrey will not support you if you decide to show any further interest in this sibling group." After Morag's reply I felt very deflated. Was I ever going to find my second daughter and a sister for Shannon? Since adopting Shannon the system had changed, instead of receiving profiles through the post, we would look at children's profiles through link maker, an online website. That Saturday morning I decided that I would sign onto the link maker to see if I was drawn to any children waiting to be adopted. Suddenly I saw Hafsa, a beautiful little girl with long black hair and dark brown eyes, wearing a purple raincoat. As I read further I realised Hafsa was from Doncaster in Yorkshire. I had never shown Shannon any of the children's profiles I had looked at before, I do not know why, but that Saturday morning I ran into Shannon's

bedroom and said, "Shannon, I have found your sister." Shannon said, "Mummy, can I see a photo of her?" As I showed Shannon the photo of Hafsa, she said "Mummy, that is my sister."
"How will you feel that your sister is a different colour to you?"
"Colour does not matter, she will be my sister whatever colour she is and although I have not met her, I will love her with all my heart."
I sent an email through the link maker to Claire, Hafsa's social worker's manager and she answered immediately and said that she had met me and talked to me at the adoption day in London. Claire organised for Hafsa's social worker Josie and her foster carer Carol to come and visit me in Sunningdale for the day to tell me all about hafsa. Josie and Carol decided to travel by train from Doncaster to Sunningdale and I met them at Sunningdale station and brought them to my house for lunch. Carol was very quiet and did not tell me very much about Hafsa, the only thing that Carol did say is that Hafsa was the perfect child. I then realised that Carol did not really want to tell me very much about Hafsa and I noticed that Carol did not want to be at the meeting. As I drove them both back to the station I really did not know very much more about Hafsa ,than before they had arrived. Luckily I had decided whatever Hafsa was like, I really wanted Hafsa to be my forever daughter.
In January 2017 I was invited with Shannon to go and stay in Doncaster for two weeks so that we could meet Hafsa and get to know her. We woke up very early that morning and took the train from Sunningdale to Waterloo and then jumped on the Underground to Kings Cross station where we boarded the train to Doncaster. It was a long journey and when we arrived we were met

by Claire at Doncaster station. As I had been to Doncaster before I knew what to expect, but I was not prepared for the freezing cold weather. Claire drove me to pick up my hire car, unfortunately we did not have the correct paperwork and I would not be able to hire the car. I would have to take taxis to and fro wherever we had to go. It was now very late and we were all extremely tired. Claire drove us to the hotel where we were staying and she said that she would meet at reception at nine o'clock in the morning, to drive us to Carol's house to meet Hafsa. We arrived at Carol's house and Hafsa opened the front door and said, oh hello who are you? Carol showed us through into her large lounge and offered us a cup of tea. Shannon clung onto me for dear life, as Doncaster had too many bad memories for her. Hafsa was very distant and continued to play the board game on her own, that she was playing with Carol before we had arrived. While Carol disappeared into her kitchen to make the tea. Josie, Hafsa's social worker, sat on Carol's cream leather sofa observing the situation.

It was a completely different situation and feeling for me than when I had first met Shannon in Doncaster four years earlier. Hafsa was very distant and showed no emotion, I wanted to run over to her, pick her up and give her a big hug. My gut feeling told me that Hafsa was not ready for this, it was my need and not hafsa's. Shannon and I spent the next two weeks staying at the hotel In Doncaster, travelling back and forwards to Carol's house to spend the day with Hafsa. On one occasion Hafsa wanted to stay the night with us in the hotel and social services agreed. Years later, Hafsa told me that she only wanted to stay with us in the hotel that night, so that she could have pancakes and Nutella for breakfast.

At the end of the two weeks, Shannon and I left Doncaster and went home to Sunningdale. Shannon had made a beautiful felt doll for Hafsa which Shannon named Lilly, together Shannon and I prepared Hafsa's bedroom for her and the following week Hafsa arrived.

Hafsa travelled on the train from Doncaster with her foster carer Carol and Carol's friend Katie, who was also a foster carer. When they arrived at Sunningdale station they all jumped into a taxi which took them to the Rose and Crown in Sunninghill. Carol had got muddled, as I had booked to have lunch at the Rose and Crown on Sunday, before Carol and Katie were due to go home to Doncaster. Carol ordered another taxi from the Rose and Crown and finally they all arrived at Beech Hill Road.

Hafsa was not allowed to go to school that term and had to stay at home with me, so that we could start to form an attachment with each other. Hafsa was very quiet, very distant and always wanted to please me in whatever she did. I always remember what Carol had told me at our first meeting, Hafsa was the perfect child. At bedtime when I went to tuck Hafsa up and say goodnight, Hafsa told me my hands were cold and she did not want me to touch her. I was devastated that I was unable to hug or kiss Hafsa, although later on I understood why.

Shannon was very volatile and very loving, when Hafsa arrived she was very polite and helpful but very distant. Shannon was very happy to have a new sister and Hafsa was very happy to have someone to play with. Hafsa started HolyTrinity School in the summer term at the end of year two. Shannon was now in year six and busy studying for her SATS. In September 2018 Shannon started secondary school in Bracknell.

When Shannon was in year four, I decided that I would approach the school to start an after school Dance Club, the school agreed that I could start my club in the Spring term. It was a huge success and it continued for many years. Little did I know that this is where I would first meet my third daughter, Summer. It was the Summer term of 2018 and a new little girl with long auburn hair and turquoise blue eyes had just joined Hafsa's class in year three, her name was Summer. That day Hafsa and Summer ran out of school together and the minute I saw Summer, I remember thinking to myself what a lovely little girl. Hafsa said, Mummy I have just met a new friend called Summer and she is going to be adopted by her forever mummy just like me. Hafsa and Summer sat next to each other in class and became good friends. One Wednesday afternoon Summer came into the school hall and asked if she could join the Dance Club with Hafsa. I told Summer that she would need to have her parents permission first. That evening her parents emailed me and the following week Summer joined the Dance Club. Summer loved to dance and really enjoyed Dance Club with Hafsa and her friends.

In 2019 I had decided to have a loft conversion done on our Victorian cottage in Beech Hill Road, so that I could apply to adopt my third child, as I had always wanted to have four children and Shannon and Hafsa loved the idea of having another sister. I contacted Surrey Social Services to see if they could approve me to adopt another child, unfortunately their response was extremely negative and they told me that it was far too early to even think of adopting a third child. Deciding not to give up I went through every adoption agency in the country and finally in June 2019 Adopters for Adopters (AFA) gave me an interview, which I passed and I was allocated my new social worker Ogo. I had passed my DBS check and my medical for the third time and Ogo had started writing my prospective adopters report (PAR).

Then one Sunday morning at nine o'clock there was a knock on the door. As I answered the door, Shannon and Hafsa were half asleep and I told them to quickly get dressed as Ogo was standing on the front door step. I invited Ogo in and offered her a cup of tea, feeling very confused why she would not want to be with her own children at 9am on a Sunday morning. I thought to myself that Ogo must be extremely dedicated to her job. Shannon and Hafsa rushed downstairs half dressed to see who it was. Ogo explained that she had come to individually interview Shannon and Hafsa to see how they felt about sharing a mummy with another sister. We sat down and ate our breakfast and then Ogo took Hafsa into the lounge and started asking her questions. The first question was, "Hafsa would you like to change your name," and Hafsa replied "NO!" Then Ogo asked Hafsa if she would have any triggers if mummy adopted another child? Hafsa replied "NO!"

"Hafsa, would you be able to share a mummy with another sister", and Hafsa replied "YES!"

"Can I share this information with mummy?" and Hafsa replied "NO!"

Shannon was asked to complete a worksheet with Ogo to see if she wanted a sister and if she could cope with having a sister. When Shannon was also asked if she wanted to share this information with mummy, Shannon also replied "NO!" To this day both Hafsa and Shannon do not know why they said no. The following week I had another visit from Ogo, to say that I could no longer adopt through AFA. I was shocked and annoyed, surely having two successful adoptions was enough evidence, any child being interviewed at 9am on a Sunday morning after a busy week at school would be thrown by this unexpected visit.

I decided that I was going to write a formal letter of complaint to AFA. This was completely unfair and I did not deserve to be treated this way. My formal complaint went to AFA's agency decision maker which was overturned and I was allocated another social worker Karen.

During this time, Summer had invited Hafsa to her house for a playdate after school. Hafsa had a lovely time and really enjoyed Summer's company. I then invited Summer to our house for a playdate with Hafsa. Shannon was also very excited that Summer was coming to play and it was lovely to see the three girls getting on so well together. Summer's forever Mummy came to collect her and while the girls were playing Barbies and singing and dancing together upstairs, Summer's Forever Mummy broke down crying, "What is the matter?" I asked her.

"I am finding the adoption process really hard to cope with." I gave her a big hug and told her not to give up, as it was an extremely difficult process and I was here for her if she needed me. Weeks passed and I was continuing with my adoption process to be an approved adopter for my third daughter, although I had still not met Karen. We spoke regularly on the phone in order for her to complete my PAR. It was the summer term 2019 and Holy Trinity School Sports Day, Hafsa was very excited as she had been chosen to take part in the running race and she came second. After Sports day had finished and everyone was clearing up, Summer came running over to congratulate Hafsa. As the girls began to play, Summer's forever Mummy came over to talk to me and wanted me to know that she and her husband had decided that they could no longer adopt Summer and that they were going to put her back into care. I was completely shell shocked and could not believe what she was saying, how could they do this? This was a lifelong commitment they had entered into, it was not a dog that you could just take back to the RSPCA, this was a human being, a young innocent child who had ended up in this dreadful situation through no fault of her own. I kept this to myself and did not tell anyone. In the back of my mind I was thinking, what if I could adopt Summer?

Shannon and Hafsa Dressing up.

First meeting with Hafsa

Chapter 8

It was early one Sunday morning and I was lying in bed in my newly decorated bedroom in the loft conversion which had been built, so that my new adopted daughter could move into the spare bedroom downstairs. I could hear Hafsa and Shannon playing happily together and the birds singing outside my bedroom window. It had been a difficult week at Cranleigh school as I had found out there was going to be a new Head of Dance, as Kate and her family were relocating to Liverpool. I had been teaching at Cranleigh School for ten years and thoroughly enjoyed it. I would love to have been Head of Dance and after my ten years of hard work and dedication to the school, I really thought I deserved the position. The headmaster, Mike Wilson and his wife Carolyn were also leaving to go to teach in the new Cranleigh School in Abu Dhabi. That Monday morning I drove to school as usual to teach my ballet classes. When I arrived I was told that Liz would no longer be playing for me, she would now be playing for Alex, the new RAD teacher. I would be teaching my Cecchetti ballet classes from now on in the small, carpeted music studio and I would have to use a CD player. I knew they could not sack me as I had done nothing wrong, but this was the school's way of casting me out, as the new Head of Dance was also bringing her pupils with her to join the school. The school now wanted RAD ballet classes; there were not enough dance students to run Cecchetti and RAD ballet classes alongside each other. What was I going to do?

I woke up very early the next morning and out of the blue I decided to Google dance schools for sale, there it was right in front of my very eyes, a beautiful detached victorian dance school for sale in Devon. I called the estate agent immediately and asked if I could arrange an appointment to go to Devon and view it. Lynn the estate agent was shocked, she had only put the dance school on the market ten minutes before I rang! It was meant to be. My stepmother had very kindly offered to look after the girls for the day, while I took the train from Sunningdale to Torquay. Lynn met me at the station and drove me along the seafront to the dance school. As we turned the corner there in front of me was the most beautiful building, I fell in love with the building straight away and just knew I had to buy it. Lynn rang the doorbell and Marisa the owner of the school greeted us warmly and invited us in. I walked through the front door and up the grand oak staircase, in front of me was the most beautiful stained glass window, it took me back to my days at Hurst Lodge School. As we walked from room to room with their high ornate ceilings and deep wooden skirting boards, I lost count of how many rooms there were. Could I really live here on my own with my three children and run the dance school? As Marisa showed us downstairs, I opened the door and in front of my very eyes was a lovely dance studio with a wooden dance floor, mirrors, barres and a large bay window. We then went though into another ballet studio which had a Harlequin floor. I could not wait to get home and tell Shannon and Hafsa all about the Dance School in Devon.

Any house move is a major decision for a family, moving away from family and friends, a change of school for the girls and having only recently adopted Hafsa the previous year, my head was in a complete jumble. I had so many thoughts whizzing through my head. The girls had had many moves in their short lives already. What would the impact be on the girls, would I be able to cope on my own looking after the girls and running the dance school?

In May 2018 I decided I would take the girls to Devon to see the dance school. We stayed at the Anchorage Hotel opposite the dance school so that we could see how it felt living in the area.

Hafsa loved the idea of living in Devon and she was amazed at how large the building was, Shannon was apprehensive but happy to move to Devon. We came home and I decided to put my house on the market to see if anyone wanted to buy it.

I told my social worker Kate and Liz, the lovely lady I was working with from Barnados children society. Although both professionals were supportive about me following my dream I could tell by their body language that they were concerned and so was I. I had a couple of offers on my house but I could not achieved the amount I needed in order to buy the dance school, so i decided to take my house off the market and stay in Sunningdale. That summer, we stayed in England as Hafsa did not have a passport and I decided to have a dance studio built at the end of our garden so that I could teach from home. The girls loved playing and dancing in the dance studio, having it at the end of the garden was ideal as I could keep a watchful eye on the girls playing from the kitchen window. I decided to leave Cranleigh School after ten years and I applied for a teaching Job at an ISTD dance school in Wokingham, about half an hours drive from our home. Olivia, who owned the dance school, was going to move

with her husband to Dubai that Summer for three years and wanted me to run her school for her while she was away. As I could no longer afford to buy the dance school in Devon, I suggested to Olivia that I could buy her school. Olivia agreed and invited me to observe her classes and teach the students during the Summer term before she left for Dubai. The students were busy preparing for their end of year performance of Copelia at South Hill Park Theatre in Bracknell.
I had brought tickets for myself, Shannon and Hafsa to watch the students last performance of Copelia, as Olivia was going to announce that the dance school would be changing hands, after the performance had finished. Sadly we never made that performance as my father was taken seriously ill and admitted to Wexham park hospital in Slough. I called my good friend Julie, Shannon's Godmother, who dropped everything and immediately drove over from Byfleet to Sunningdale to support myself and the girls. As soon as Julie arrived we rushed to the hospital. We ran through the long corridors, and found Daddy lying in his hospital bed, his breathing heavy and infrequent. The palliative nurse had told us not to give daddy any food or drink. I held his hand and sang to him, Shannon recited his favourite poem, "The Highwayman," and Hafsa told him about the things her class had done at school, all the while he was whispering, "Thank you." We went home in the early hours of Saturday morning, and tried to sleep, but it was no good. We were in the car at 7am, driving to the hospital. When we arrived, Daddy had his eyes open, and all of my family were there. We stayed the whole day, myself and the girls barely leaving his side. Even though Daddy was not allowed to eat, he asked for food, and the nurse relented and

allowed us to give him yogurt. My step-mother had now left the room, upset and distraught, and Shannon and Hafsa helped me to feed Daddy. But it was all too much for the girls to cope with, and Vicky, my good friend, offered to have Shannon and Hafsa to stay with her for a couple of nights and drove over to Sunningdale the following morning to collect them, whilst I went to see Daddy. The following day, Daddy had gone into a coma, I carried on singing to him and reciting his favourite poetry, and on the 15th July 2019 at Wexham Park Hospital, my Daddy died in his sleep. I was there as he took his last breath, holding his hand always, and then, he was gone. I never realised Daddy was so poorly, daddy was never ill he would wake up very early every morning, always happy and singing as he shaved, covering his face with Gillette creamy white shaving foam, that looked and felt like the white whipped cream mummy would always put in between the layers of her delicious black forest gateau, not forgetting to save a big dollop for the top. Daddy would always put a dab of his shaving foam on my nose, as he sang his favourite songs, "Daddy wouldn't buy me a bow wow," and recited his poetry "Johnathon Joe had a mouth like an O," or "Going Downhill on a Bicycle." Daddy loved singing and poetry. He was a very kind and caring man, never saw bad in anyone or anything, he could not stand confrontation and would always turn a blind eye, rather than stand up for himself. I remember we had just moved to Manor Farm in Binfield, we had left our modern detached five bedroomed house in Greenways Drive, Sunningdale for a large detached run down farmhouse with six and a half acres of land and a rippling stream running through our garden. The farmhouse had a beautiful inglenook fireplace with alcoves built into the walls on either side of the fireplace with red velvet cushioned seats that one could sit on. I loved sitting on those seats watching the flames of the fire dance and crackle against the wood that daddy had chopped that day, from the many deserted tree trunks in our enormous field. Daddy loved making fires, something he always enjoyed and continued to do until the end of his life. Mummy and Daddy struggled with the workload at Manor Farm as well as looking after us four children, Daddy was always exhausted when he got home from his butcher shop, it was not so easy for Nanna and Grandad to drive from Byfleet to Binfield, as it had been when they drove before to visit us in Sunningdale, as they were getting older now and it was a long way for them to drive, especially in the dark. As there was a lot of building work to be done at Manor Farm, Daddy employed Derek the builder who had always done a lot of repairs for him at the butcher shops, Daddy owned seven shops in total with his elder brother Don.

Over the years Derek and his wife Jo had become family friends. Since I was very young I had never liked Derek, as he was very bossy. Mummy had already told us that she and Daddy were going to get divorced , which I did not know and nor did Daddy that Mummy and Derek were having an affair. I will never forget that evening when Daddy came home from work and the telephone rang and he answered it. It was Jo, Derek's wife, who told him that Mummy and Derek were having an affair. Daddy put the phone down and fell on the settee with grief, he burst out crying, "Why would your mother want to leave me after I have given her four children?" I had never seen Daddy cry before and this was the saddest day of my life.

As well as the very sad memories at Manor Farm I have very fond memories of my dearest great Nanna Holland, Nanna Willis's mother who had taught me how to knit and brought me my very first red suitcase out of her Gratten's catalouge, I felt so grown up owning my own suitcase in my very favourite colour, red. I can see Nanna Holland now sitting upright at the end of the ercol cream fake fur settee, which had two pull out wooden tables, one each end, with a Players weights cigarette hanging out of her mouth. With her tarnished yellow stained fingers, she had lost half of one of her fingers during world war two when she worked at Vickers, making bullets for guns in their factory. Grandad Willis also worked at Vickers with Nanna Holland in the drawing office, he was part of the team that drew the very first designs for Concorde. Nanna Holland told me that she had got her finger caught in the machine at Vickers when she was making the bullets. I loved listening to Nanna Holland's stories of times gone by as she taught me to knit. Very often a piece of ash would fall from her cigarette onto her lap, which she would quickly brush away into her ashtray. Grandad would sit with us in the front room with a Cigarette hanging out of his mouth watching football or horse racing on a Saturday afternoon. I loved spending time with my grandparents, they were such wonderful people with great character.

I always loved nanna holland teaching me how to knit, I knew she would eventually offer me a piece of her nut brittle or marathon, which she always kept at the bottom of her knitting bag. One dreadfully dark day Nanna felt poorly and took herself to bed.I was eleven at the time and was downstairs in the kitchen with nanna

Willis and mummy. Suddenly there was an enormous bang coming from upstairs. We all ran as fast as we could to find nanna holland slumped over the bathroom sink, she had got up to go to the toilet and collapsed holding onto the bathroom sink. Mummy stayed with nanna holland and I went downstairs with nanna willis, while she called Doctor Dickson, our family doctor. He arrived very quickly and they managed to get nanna back into bed. Nanna had had a cerebral haemorrhage and the doctor told mummy that if he had tried to resuscitate nanna, she could end up being a cabbage for the rest of her life. Mummy came downstairs after speaking with the doctor and told us what he had said. We all went upstairs to nanna's bedroom and little did I know that day that would be my final goodbye to Nanna Holland. As I walked through the bedroom door, I had no idea what was going on. Nanna's face was taught and twisted. She was asleep, I focused on the picture of Jesus, she always kept on her bedside table inscripted with the lord is my shepherd underneath. Nanna Holland loved that picture, it meant so much to her. Mummy was holding Nanna Willis in her arms and they were both crying. I was holding nanna holland's hand and just wished she would open her eyes to speak to me once more. Nanna Holland never did wake up again, I was heartbroken and could not stop crying. I had never lost anyone or anything I loved before. At that time I was considered too young to go to Nanna Holland's funeral which was held at St Mary's Church in Byfleet. I never forgave my mummy for not letting me go to nanna holland's funeral, as I wanted so much to say my final goodbye. Nanna was buried in the same grave as Grandad Holland. Grandad Holland had died before I was born. I was told he was an accomplished pianist and loved to play the piano. He also invented the car Indicator and reclining seat. Unfortunately he could not afford to have his inventions patented and someone else stole his ideas. It was my thirteenth birthday party, we were all sitting at the dining room table, mummy was just about to light the candles on my birthday cake when the phone rang, mummy put the matches down and went to answer the phone. The look on my mother's face was of pure sadness, as she entered the dining room, to tell us that auntie Esther had just died. I was shocked and saddened, how could auntie Esther die on my thirteenth birthday. How unfair was that! Nanna Holland had died and now Auntie Esther. My grandparents had always believed in superstitions and told me that things happen in three, I thought to myself who was going to die next? My great Grandmother Nanna Elliot, grandad's mother, had lived with Auntie Esther for many years and they had both always looked after me while my parents and grandparents were working. I have such fond memories of the wonderful times I spent with Nanna Elliot and Auntie Esther at their ground floor maisonette in Oyster Lane, Byfleet. They had a beautiful garden and although it was small, it was full of the most beautiful red, pink and yellow roses. They loved spending time in their garden with me and if I close my eyes now, I can still smell the beautiful scent of those roses and see the bruises on nanna Elliots arms, where she would catch herself on the rose thorns. Whenever I stayed with them I would be treated to a bowl of cold, Ambrosia rice pudding, straight from the tin. Nanna Elliot and Auntie Esther had their own bedrooms and I loved looking through her draws to see what I could find. As I opened the draw it was full of mothballs, horrible scented balls scattered amongst their bloomers to keep the moths from eating their clothes. As well as tins of Ambrosia rice pudding, there was always a fruit bowl of black bananas on the dining room table. Nanna believed that a banana was not ready to eat unless it was black and then she would burn her toast before spreading her black bananas on top. Next to the fruit bowl was a small fake orange tree plant, that I always believed was real although I never did try those oranges. Every evening before bed ,Nanna Elliott would have her tipple of Johnny Walker's scotch whiskey. When Auntie Esther died, Nanna Elliot and her little white poodle Teddy, that we had given to her when my sister Vanessa was two, moved in with nanna and grandad at 141 Church Road.

In September 2019 The Lewis Academy of Dancing reopened its doors again at Emmbrook Village Hall. After daddy died life was never the same again, a big shining light went out in our lives, I was heartbroken but I knew that daddy was pleased that I was buying the dance school in Wokingham, I remember him saying, it is a lovely drive from Sunningdale To Wokingham along the country roads, you will enjoy that drive with the girls.

Shannon was deversated, Grandad had been the first man she had ever trusted in her life and found letting go of him extremely difficult. Hafsa did not have a strong attachment to daddy, as she had not known him very long and most of that time daddy had been very poorly with Pulmonary Fibrosis. I postponed our holiday to Corfu that Summer and for the girls sake, I felt as a family we should try to continue with some sort of normality and after daddy's funeral we flew out to Corfu for the rest of the Summer holidays. In September the girls returned to school and I started teaching Cecchetti Ballet at The Lewis Academy of Dancing. The students at the dance school had previously taken their ISTD ballet exams with Olivia and now they would be studying for their Cecchetti ballet exams with me. The following term in March 2020 covid broke out and I had to close the dance school. That September I opened the dance school again, not at Emmbrook Village Hall but on zoom. Having never done zoom in my life before I did not know where to start, but I knew I just had to do it to save my dance school. Alice Jervis very kindly came over to my house and taught Shannon and I how to teach a ballet class on zoom. My small kitchen at Beech Hill Road was transformed into a dance studio. Shannon and Hafsa were a fantastic help, as well as helping me on zoom they also demonstrated the exercises on the wooden kitchen floor. The kitchen chairs became our ballet barres and off we went into the world of Zoom. When covid broke out I also started homeschooling the girls, as they were not allowed to go to school and in the afternoons I would teach my Cecchetti ballet classes on Zoom. At this time I was still continuing to focus on trying to adopt my third daughter Summer. Unfortunately due to covid the adoption process slowed down, then finally in August 2020 we drove to Barnstable in Devon to meet Summer and her foster career. After our long drive to Devon in Lily, our twenty year old little white Nissan Micra, we arrived at Summer's foster carer's house. I had never driven to Devon before in my life, it was a hot August day and the motorways were chock-a- block. As we drove around the corner into the estate where Summer was staying with her foster carer, Summer was sitting on the front door step waiting to greet us. Summer's social worker invited us in. As I walked through the door into the lounge, I was in complete shock. The house was dark and depressing, all the curtains were closed and the foster carer was dressed from head to toe in black. She greeted us loftly, and due to her size, she slumped down onto the black, leather sofa. There was an awkward silence. It felt like hours before she offered us a drink. Then she reluctantly went to make some tea and came back, and gave it to me. As we had travelled so far, and had not been able to stop on the way, it would have been nice to have been offered something to eat, even if it was a biscuit. The social worker sat at the dining room table, tapping away at the laptop in front of her. There was little conversation. Summer came bounding up to me, and offered me a Lindt chocolate truffle. She then proceeded to eat the entire box herself, both Summer's foster carer and her social worker completely ignoring her. In the end, I told her to stop eating them, and under the watchful eyes of everyone in the room, Summer put the box down, reluctantly.

After our first visit, which only lasted for two days, Summer's foster carer put in an official complaint about me, as she wanted to continue fostering Summer and not to give her up for adoption. She complained that I had not given Summer a Mcflurry at McDonalds, that Shannon had anger issues and that she did not agree with me giving Summer baths. This meant that Summer did not come to live with us until 11th November 2020, Eleven months after I had first applied to adopt Summer. On the 11th November the day Summer was due to move in with us, Summer decided to run away to her friend's house and the police were called, the social workers arrived and Summer refused to get into the car. Eventually the social worker's managed to bribe Summer into their car with three packets of sweets and a promise of a McDonalds on the way to Sunningdale. As soon as Summer arrived, she ran upstairs to play Barbies with Shannon and Hafsa and I entertained Summer's foster carer and two social workers, until they promptly left to drive back to Devon.

Before they all left, I called Summer downstairs to say her goodbyes. Summer was more interested in playing Barbies upstairs with Shannon and Hafsa, rather than saying goodbye to her foster carer forever.

The following month in December 2020 I organised my first Cecchetti exam session, with my new students at Emmbrook Village Hall. The students had never done Cecchetti ballet before, as they were ISTD ballet trained with Olivia.

I was fortunate that the government took the country out of Covid lockdown, to enable us to have our exam session that December. We all had a wonderful day, our examiner was Lisa Christian and Liz Hewson was our pianist. The students gained excellent results, the majority passing their ballet exams with distinction. Summer had now joined the Dance School and was working hard towards her Grade One Cecchetti, which she was going to take at our next exam session in July with our Cecchetti examiner Alison Jenner.

After our first Christmas together with Summer, due to Covid 19 we went back into lockdown and back onto Zoom. Having a lot of time on my hands and not being able to travel anywhere, I kept thinking about the Dance School in Devon and was inquisitive to find out what had happened to it. One April morning in 2021, I decided to call Lynn the estate agent, to find out if the Dance School was still for sale. Lynn said that the owners had decided to take the Dance School off the market and were now thinking of selling it as a residential property. Lynn asked me if I was still interested in buying the Dance School. Without thinking, I said yes, what had I done? I then decided to put my house in Sunningdale on the market again. Due to my next door neighbours having a million pixies and gnomes on our garden fence, which I could not remove, there had been hardly any interest in my house, so the estate agent had advised me to lower the price. After daddy died all our lives completely changed, there were family disagreements due to daddy's will being lost and having already been through a huge turmoil in my life when my parents got divorced, there was no way i was going to put my three daughters and myself through the stress of my families disagreements. What I did not think of, is how social services would react to me moving Summer back to Devon, when she had lived in Devon for the majority of her life and had had both of her foster placements in Devon. I then needed to make a huge decision, having been alone with my three daughters during both Covid lockdowns with no support, I had decided that we could move to Devon and buy the Dance School. That summer, we all flew out to Corfu together. Summer had never been abroad before, let alone on an aeroplane. Summer was so exciting and so were we, as we had not been to Corfu for the last two years due to travel restrictions. However we still had not received permission from social services and were not sure if we were going to go at all. Being optimistic I packed our bags and drove to Heathrow airport to have our covid tests done, luckily we were all negative. I then started to complete our passenger locator forms, while I was in the middle of completing them, the phone rang and it was Summer's social worker. At the eleventh hour, to tell me that her manager had given us all permission to go. I had had my students Cecchetti ballet exams at Emmbrook Village Hall the day before we left for Corfu and I cannot tell you how exhausting it was trying to get everything organised for our holiday and not even knowing if we were definately going! As we boarded our plane, I was just about to put my mobile phone on aeroplane mode. When it started ringing, I answered it and it was the estate agent who told me that I had had an offer on my house, an offer I could not refuse if I wanted to buy the Dance School and move to Devon. I switched my mobile phone off and we flew to Corfu. That summer when we were in Corfu, I was finally approved to adopt Summer. Little did I know that when I told my social worker at Adopters For Adopters about our move to Devon and how it had come about, she did not believe me and was convinced that I had engineered the whole move to Devon behind her back. I then received a letter from the agency decision maker from Adopters for Adopters to say that they would no longer support me in adopting Summer. It was a huge shock! The move to Devon was a no brainer. The Dance School was set in a quiet, beautiful location in between two parks and in walking distance to shops, restaurants and most importantly for all of us two stunning beaches Oddicombe and Babacombe.

Since Covid I had been home schooling all three of my daughters and when the government said it was time to return to school. The girls said that they felt relaxed and happier at home and could learn more as they did not have any pressure or bullying affecting their behaviour. Shannon said to me, " Mummy, if you send me to the best school in the world, I would still be happier, healthier and learn a lot more at home."

And Shannon was right, since that day all three of my daughters are home schooled, they have all gained excellent social skills through moving to the Dance School in Devon. They all love to dance and interact with their friends. It also enables us to do a lot more travelling, which has really broadened the girls' horizons and given us a stronger attachment as a family.

With Nanna Eliot and Auntie Esther

Hafsa and Grandad on her Adoption Day

Shannon and Hafsa at Covent Garden   Shannon and Grandad

A Family outing when I was 2

Chapter 9

We flew back from Corfu on Monday 20th September and exchanged contracts on Friday 24th September and completed and moved to Devon on Tuesday 28th September 2021. That Summer before we returned to England, I prepared the girls for our move to Devon. I had an excellent solicitor Jonathon Perry from XYZ law, who I had found online while I was in Corfu.

Mr Mover was brilliant and himself and his son moved us from Sunningdale to Devon, the heros in our move were Shannon, Hafsa and Summer, who were really excited to move to Devon. When we arrived home from Corfu, with no support or help from anyone in our family we packed and we packed box after box, until all our belongings and memories from the last ten years were on route to Devon. Our Little white, twenty year old Dahatsui Hijet Colin, named after my daddy, was on his first motorway journey since we had brought him earlier that year.

Little did I know if he would actually make it to Devon.

Very early that morning, Mr Mover and his son arrived and one by one they carried all our boxes that we had spent the last week packing, into the van, followed by our furniture and what we could not fit in the van, we left behind. We said goodbye to Beech Hill Road and put all our precious things in Colin and started our drive to Devon. The day we left, there was a petrol shortage and having filled up Colin's tank the night before, I was worried that we would not have enough petrol to get to Devon. We had a lovely drive to Devon, singing and joking all the way and Shannon being a history buff nearly deafened me when she squealed, "Look, there's Stonehenge!" Just past Stonehenge I saw a small garage with petrol and a queue of cars ascending down the road. I decided to stop and join the queue. I jumped out of Colin and filled his tank up, as I got back in Colin to drive away my foot kept slipping off the clutch and the impatient lady behind me started honking her horn. However hard I tried, it was no good. My foot just kept slipping. I could not think what it was. Luckily I had a spare pair of Jazz shoes in the boot, so I quickly changed my shoes and continued our drive to Devon. Jokingly on the way, I said to the girls I would not be surprised if the social workers were waiting for us when we arrived at the Dance School. There was a heavy downpour of rain as we turned the corner and onto the road leading to the Dance School. As we entered the driveway all the windows on Colin were steamed up and as I wiped my side window I saw a black car parked next to us. Oh look girls it is Lynn the estate agent, she has arrived with the keys to our new home. I jumped out of Colin to let Hafsa and Summer out of the back and to my horror there were two of Summer's social workers sitting inside the black car. I thought to myself why do they need to visit us now, the very day we are moving into our new home.

Just then, Lynn the estate agent arrived with the keys for our new home as the previous owners had already left. I opened the front door and kindly invited the social workers in. The girls had suddenly disappeared as they were all so excited to explore their new home, or escape from the social workers. In haste, the social workers went off to find the girls. I paused for a moment after our long journey and looked up at the magnificent stained glass window in front of me, towering above me. Had I really done it? Finally after thirty six years of teaching in cold, draughty village halls, logging heavy CD players around with me, lifting and erecting and dismantling heavy portable ballet barres, tables and chairs, storing dance uniforms and show costumes in the back of my car. What a huge achievement I now owned my very own Dance School in Devon. The overweight teenager who had been told by Mrs Merrick while at Hurst Lodge School that dancing was not a proper job had proved it. In one's life you can achieve anything if you put your mind to it and never ever give up! The girls came running into the hallway, mummy came and saw the dance studios. They are amazing. As I wandered into the first dance studio, standing on the beautiful wooden dance floor, the girls dancing ahead of me while looking at themselves in front of the two very large studio mirrors, the social workers appeared and asked if they could take photographs of us all standing at the ballet barres together. They then offered to go and get some shopping at Lidl for us, which was a great help as I was so exhausted mentally and physically.

For the last ten years I have been working with social services and many social workers and their managers from all over England. Through my unconditional love, dedication and passion to adopt my three amazing, beautiful girls. I have attended numerous training courses, read a million books and spent hours talking and connecting to other adopters who have followed a similar start in their adoption journey to myself. Every parent's journey is completely different, not one of them is the same, as each child is unique. Having started my journey in my life with my birth parents who later went on to get divorced. I also was due to be a birth parent myself, my family were very excited they bought me a cot and a pram, my dear Nanna Willis started to knit baby clothes and then I was due for my scan. I will never forget the day my mother drove me to St Peter's Hospital in Chertsey. I was scared and nervous , I had never done this before a child was growing inside me and I was alone, the child's father had run off offering to pay for the best abortion, there is no best abortion for a woman in love with a man and carring his baby.

My mother, having had six children, had done all of this before, but this was my very first time. We arrived at the hospital, sitting in the waiting room, the door opened and the nurse called my name. I went in alone, my mother anxiously waiting outside. The nurse smoothed some gel all over my stomach and then turned on the ultrasound machine. I looked at the screen at the side of me. I could not believe there was a baby inside me, a beating heart, a new life. The nurse then turned to me and told me to lie still while she went to fetch another nurse. I was scared, I could feel in my gut that something was seriously wrong, I thought to myself what could be wrong. I had seen my baby's heart beating.

The nurses returned with a solemn look on their faces, "We are sorry to tell you but your baby's legs are not developing properly. If you go ahead and give birth, the baby could die as well as yourself. It is too late for you to have an abortion, so you will have to go into labour." I got dressed and left the room in shock. My mother waiting outside greeted me, having told my mother I burst into floods of tears and then pulled myself together, like my mother had always taught me to do. As we were leaving the hospital, my mother turned to me and said, Oh darling it just was not meant to be.

Since I can remember, I always wanted to be a mother and have my own family and if I was not able for any reason to have my own birth children, I was definitely going to adopt. There are so many children in the world waiting to be adopted who need forever families to feel loved, safe and secure.

When you live in a birth family, abusive or not, you grow up thinking, "This is the way everyone grows up". You are sheltered so no one outside can rescue you, and you have to learn to survive very fast. When you attend school for the first time, you look at all of the happy children, who are not scared of running up to their parents after school, do not have to worry if there will be enough food on the table, or have to defend themselves against aggressive behaviour. When you are taken into care, you are placed on a plateau that causes people to pity you. Everything you had taught yourself to do is of no use anymore, and instead of being neglected by adults, you are constantly being badgered, pestered, told that you are good or bad and made to fill in sheets of paper with questions such as, "How much do you like school?", or "How happy have you been this week?" You put up with endless disruption to your daily life and you feel like you are an experiment, with certain regulations, and being analysed by people every day who know more about you than you know about yourself. To then go to an Adoptive family is a bigger change, and by this stage, you cannot cope with change. You are feral, have a deranged mindset, and believe that everyone is out to get you. The adoptive family is different. You move to a neighbourhood where no one knows you, you live in a safe environment and you can start again. Only after the adoption is finalised will you feel relieved that no one can take you away. But through that relief, your anger and damage comes out, and your new parents are tested to the limit. You push every button, just to make sure that they love you, and one day, everything falls into place. When you are in care, you get invited to so many playdates and parties, that you are very busy every weekend. It is a way of people showing how sorry they are for you, and trying to make you feel happy and accepted. The happiness does not last for long, though. The reason why it feels different to be in an adopted family, in care and in a birth family, is because in a birth family, no one cares about you; in care, you are fussed over so much that you cannot cope with it, but in a forever home with your adopted family, you get just the right amount of attention and care to make you feel safe.

During the national covid lockdown, which started on 23rd March 2020, I was alone with my two daughters Shannon and Hafsa. I had no support and we were only allowed to leave the house once a day for food shopping and exercise. We were all terrified, although I knew I was the girl's rock and could not show them how afraid and worried I was. Daily I would follow the national news hour by hour, we had no idea what would happen next. When I did my weekly shop at Waitrose in Sunningdale, which cost me an absolute fortune as it was the only supermarket near to our house, I would leave Shannon and Hafsa in the car so that they did not catch the virus.

On the first day Covid was announced, I sent the girls to school all wearing their new scuba diving masks that Vicky had very kindly bought the girls for Christmas. These masks were for our summer holidays in Corfu, to enjoy diving under the Ionian blue sea, not to wear to school! Would we travel abroad again? Would we ever be able to get close to our family and friends again? Has our world and our lives changed forever? Little did I know that it was going to be the last day my daughters would ever walk into a school again. My parents, my grandparents and even my great grandparents had always believed in a good education. My parents worked very hard to be able to pay for all four of their children to have private education and attend reputable junior and senior schools. I wanted to do the same for my children and never dreamed that I would ever be homeschooling my two daughters at home around the kitchen table.

When I first adopted Shannon my social worker from PACT was dead against me sending Shannon to a private school and insisted that she should go to the local Primary School. Looking back I think she was right, I could have paid fortunes for all my daughter's education at private schools.

When we started homeschooling, I noticed that Shannon and Hafsa were so much happier, and there were fewer arguments between them. I started to take notice of the amount of things that the girls knew, as they both never really told me anything about their school day. I asked Shannon if she would like to go back to school, she said " Mummy, even if you send me to the best school in the world, I would still be happier and learn more if I stayed at home." I am so pleased that I listened to Shannon and made my own decision to homeschool my children. A decision I would never have been brave enough to make, if we had not gone through the Covid pandemic together as a family. It allowed us to spend so much quality time together, getting to know each other and enjoying each other's company. In life it is very easy to get caught up in a web not knowing which way to turn, being influenced by family, friends and the outside world and pleasing others as you travel through your life's journey. No matter what, parents want to and do what they think and feel is best for their children. By improving a little on what their parents did or did not do for them and what generations before did for their children, you have created a parenting pattern, without even realising it. Step back, break the pattern and start again; give your children a fresh start in life, one they deserve. Yes you love them, hopefully you want them, but listen to them, sit back and observe them, watch what they do and see them grow, day by day and find out who they really are. They are not you; you are not them. They are themselves and they deserve to be who they are, love them for who they are. Do not judge them against one another as they are unique in their own very special way. Please recognise this in your child as there is no such a thing as a naughty child. If your child does not turn out the way you wanted him or her to be, accept your child for who they are and they will grow and flourish and find themselves throughout their life. In the beautiful and wonderful, but sometimes dark and twisted world that we live in. Throughout history, life has changed our parental journey for the better and for the worse, recognise this and be responsible for your own judgement. Choose your own path; do not follow the path of others like sheep. My children have taught me about myself, through their trauma I have listened to them, watched them and want to learn how to heal and help them and for them to understand, what happened to them in the beginning of their lives was no fault of their own.

All of my daughters had problems fitting in with the children in the school playground. As the school bell rang for break time, Hafsa was worried that no one would want to play with her, she would secretly hug her teddy Billy, that I had put in her school rucksack that morning. Very scared and frightened that the other children would judge her, Hafsa would wander around the school playground alone wanting anyone to come and play with her. In December 2020 the country went into a second national lockdown. Summer arrived in November that year and although she had been to school in Devon throughout the first lockdown, Summer would now be homeschooled with Shannon and Hafsa. At first Summer disliked homeschooling because she enjoyed being cool with her friends at school. Summer hated being told what to do and did not like the fact that I recognized how behind she was with her school work. Having received no guidance from social services when Summer first arrived and nothing from her previous school, I soon began to realise that Summer had missed a lot of school and was far behind Hafsa, even though they were both in the same school year.

The first thing I had to do was to organise a safe and regular routine for my three daughters. The girls had been through enough in their short lives already and I did not want the national lockdown due to the Covid pandemic to affect them. I decided that I would start school work with them all in the morning around the kitchen table and in the afternoon I would teach my dance classes on zoom, which they could all join in accordingly. In the afternoons when I was not teaching, we would cook scones and cakes together and watch Escape To The Chateau and dream of the day when we would live in our own Chateau, Devon Dance Centre. As well as cooking we all loved going on walks, during Covid we walked for miles through Windsor Great Park , across Sunningdale Golf Course and on Chobham Common. I could not believe how many people bought dogs during Covid, they were everywhere. When the winter came and the days were shorter and colder , if it was pouring with rain I would take the girls on mystery tours in our little white camper van, Colin, named after my loving father. We would all sing our favourite songs and recite poetry together and stop somewhere nice for a picnic lunch. As a family we also enjoyed cycle rides and we used to cycle together from our house in Beech Hill Road to Windsor Great Park and then onto Virginia water, where we would feed the swans and ducks and dance around the 100 foot Totem Pole which was brought from British Columbia in 1958. I had never been so fit in all my life. We all really enjoyed our life as a family together during the National Covid Lockdowns and surprised ourselves how wonderful it was just being together. Once a week I would call my dear friend Glen, who lives on her own in London to see how she was getting on. We would reminisce about the wonderful memories we shared together at the Cecchetti Centre, being taught by our favourite teachers Richard Glasstone, Cara Drower, Anita Young, Eve Pettinger and many more. Glen and I had known each other for over thirty years, she had given me her phone number when I last saw her at the Barbara Geoghegan Awards at Sadlers Wells Theatre in 2019. During the first national Covid lockdown I called Glen to see if she was keeping well and from that day we now catch up regularly and she has shown a very caring constant interest in myself and my three daughters. We would also write to Heather and Richard and the girls would send them both beautiful pieces of poetry and artwork and sometimes even the odd story.

Summer's First Holiday in Corfu

Shannon, Hafsa and Summer on the beach in Devon

Chapter 10

When Covid Restrictions were lifted we could all start to see our family and friends. It felt very strange to be able to get close to one another again and sit in the same room. On the 12th December for the very first time we went to visit Heather and Richard at their home in London. We took the train from Torre station to Paddington Station, this was our very first long trip from Devon to London. When we arrived at Paddington Station we walked to Rede Place. We were all so excited and overwhelmed, when Heather opened the front door to greet us all warmly and invited us into their bright yellow lounge. Covered from wall to wall with many of Heather's wonderful drawings and works of art.

Richard asked me to bring the french fancies from their kitchen table to give to the girls. The girls' eyes popped open when they saw the plate of yellow, pink and brown petit cakes coming towards them. Feeling nervous to take one under Richard's watchful eye, they eventually chose their favourite colour cake and held it melting in their hand. I then, also feeling nervous, took the plate of remaining cakes back to the kitchen and offered to make everyone a cup of tea. As I reached up to get the brown china teapot off the high kitchen cupboard, memories came flooding back to me from my childhood, when my great Nanna Holland always had a brown china teapot on her dining room table with a brightly knitted tea cosy on top to keep the tea hot. Suddenly Richard shouted "WHERE'S MY CAKE?" I jumped to attention and quickly delivered Richard his chocolate french fancie and sat down on the settee next to the girls. Richard very kindly gave me the original manuscript that Enrico Cecchetti had written on the Cecchetti method. As well as two wonderful black and white framed photographs, one of Enrico Cecchetti and Anna Pavlova sitting in her garden at Ivy House, Golders Green. The other framed photograph was that of Vaslav Nijinsky as a young boy. Richard had wanted to give me these to put up in my new dance school in Devon and reminded me that I was very lucky to have them, as he could have given them to someone else! I had just finished making the tea and sat down, when Richard turned to the girls and asked where did you three come from? At that moment I felt very proud of my girls as they all felt safe enough and comfortable enough to tell Richard and Heather their own story one by one. After a memorable and wonderful day of chatting, it was time to catch our train back home to Devon.

It was our first Christmas in Devon and the girls had successfully auditioned for their first professional pantomime "Snow White and The Seven Dwarfs" the choreographer Jo Sexton had hired one of the dance studios at Devon Dance Centre for her rehearsals. It was lovely to watch Jo choreograph her dances for the Exmouth Pantomime and I really enjoyed watching Shannon, Hafsa and Summer rehearsing with Jo, they all danced so beautifully and their costumes were amazing. The following term I invited Jo to come and teach for me at Devon Dance Centre. When we first moved to Devon in September 2021, I started teaching adult beginner and advanced ballet classes and then one day out of the blue Nadya Lisak contacted me to ask if she could join my advanced ballet classes. It was wonderful to see Nadya again after so many years. I had also been in contact with her sister Tamara on Facebook. Tamara had heard the girls were performing in their very first professional pantomime and wanted to book tickets for herself and her daughter Alina. On New Year's Eve Tamara and Alina drove from London to Exmouth to watch the pantomime and after the performance, they both came back to our house to stay the night. On New Year's Day I invited Nadya to join us all for lunch. It was so lovely to catch up after not seeing each other for over thirty years. Being the same age, Alina and Shannon got on really well together, as they both loved dancing, Harry Potter and Billie Eilish. After our two national Covid lockdowns, it felt like our lives were getting back to some kind of normality. I had booked tickets for us all to go to Corfu, as this would be Summer's very first Greek Easter, also known as Pascha.

Greek Easter is one of the most important festivals of the year. With its lavish feasts, celebrations, dancing and religious ceremonies. It is a fantastic time to be in Greece, breathing the incense-scented air and listening to the priests plaintive chant as we walk through the darkness holding our long thin white candles, walking slowly through the mountainous alleyways of Pelekas, lit only by the glimmer of the eternal flame ferried across the sea from Jerusalems's Church of the Holy Sepulchre earlier that day. At midnight the priest cries "Xristos anesti!" Christ has risen and Costa rings the church bells wildly as the young boys in the village throw firecrackers that fizz through the darkness. The villagers scurry home to make the smoky black cross above their front doors, to bring protection for the following year. While we were in Greece the girls were busy rehearsing their choreographies for the Cecchetti Choreographic competition, which would take place at Cecil Sharp House in London on our return to England in May 2022. This was a very poignant event in our family calendar. The girls were all so excited to be taking part in the choreographic competition as it was Summers' first time and the last time Shannon and Hafsa participated in the competition was in March 2020. The competition was on a Sunday and as I was not teaching the following day, I decided to book a family room for us all at the brand new Premier Inn which was very close to Paddington Station. All three of the girls had choreographed and practised their dances in the little kitchen in Corfu. We decided what the girls' costumes were on holiday, as when we got back we would only have a week before the competition. The girls practised every day, and when they performed their dances at the competition, I was blown away. Summer and Hafsa were in the Middle section, and Shannon was in the Senior Section. Summer's Dance was "The Easter Bunny", and she got an accommodation, which was amazing as it was her first time. Hafsa's dance was inspired by the queen of hearts from Alice in Wonderland, and she called it "Off with your head". Having worn masks for the last two years due to the Covid pandemic, Hafsa forgot to take her mask off and she started her dance with her mask on her face, so the adjudicators could not see her facial expressions. She took it off halfway through her dance and was awarded the Jane Worsley cup for the best storytelling through her performance. Shannon did a dance based on the stories she had been listening to of the Ukrainian Refugees, and named it "Refugee". Shannon was awarded the Felicity Jaffe Shield for the most expressive solo. All of the girls got an award, I was so proud of them all. They were all amazing, and each one of them stood out like a shining light on the stage. After the competition we took a red double decker London bus back to our hotel and as it was a warm summer's evening we had a picnic in Little Venice watching the boats floating up the river.

The next morning we all got up early and had a delicious breakfast. The girls really enjoyed it as they could eat as much as they liked. After breakfast we took the bus to Covent Garden as I had booked tickets for us all to watch the Royal Ballet Company perform a triple bill, Choreographed by Sir Fredrick Ashton. On our way to the Opera House I had arranged to meet our dear friend Glen at the dance shop in Drury Lane, as I had bought a ticket for her. Shannon and Hafsa were so excited as they were going to have their pointe shoes fitted at the dance shop. Glen arrived as the girls were trying on their pointe shoes and sat down on the soft velvet settee as Summer danced around the shop. It was so lovely to see Glen again and for her to meet Summer for the first time.

We all left the dance shop and weaved through the bustling cobbled streets to The Royal Opera House and took our seats for our very first live performance since the beginning of Covid of Scénes De Ballet, A Month in the Country and Rhapsody.

It was wonderful to be in the Opera House again, listening to the orchestra and watching Francesca Hayward and Cesar Corrales performing together in three works by the company's founding choreographer, Frederick Ashton.

We all thoroughly enjoyed the performance and after saying goodbye to Glen, we walked to Piccadilly Circus and took the bus back to Paddington to visit Richard and Heather before our long journey back to Devon.

On Sunday 22nd May 2022 I attended the Centenary celebrations at Cecchetti Day, which was held at The Royal Ballet School in Covent Garden. I was so pleased that Richard and Heather Glasstone wanted to come to Cecchetti Day and Richard asked me if I could help them, which I was honoured to do. I had also invited Glen and Nadya, whose sister Tamara very kindly offered to have the girls for me. It was a very hot day and Tamara decided after strolling around Covent Garden with the girls in the morning, that she would take them back to her house in the afternoon to watch a movie.

Cecchetti Day finished at around five o'clock and after seeing Heather and Richard to their taxi, I met up with Tamara and the girls outside The Opera House. That night we stayed at Premier Inn in London again, as I had promised the girls that the following morning, I would take them to The British Museum to see the Egyptian artefacts. The girls found it fascinating walking from room to room with so much to see and a lot to learn. It was a real treat for me as well, just watching and listening to them all during our visit.

It was our first summer in Devon and a very short one as I had booked to take the girls to Corfu in July for two months. I had Invited my sister Vanessa and her husband David to come and stay with us, to share food and fun as part of Her Majesty The Queen's Platinum Jubilee celebrations. I decided to paint the guest room white, to give it a fresh new look from the dirty cream magnolia that it was before, while Shannon was watching one of her favourite films downstairs Harry Potter and the Half Blood Prince and Hafsa and Summer were playing The Game of Life in the playroom. The girls could not believe that by the time the film had finished , I had completely finished painting the guest room, apart from the odd streak here and there, which I quickly resolved by hanging beautiful pictures up, that I had purchased previously from the numerous charity shops that we have in Babbacombe. With the curtains hung and the bed made we all headed outside into the garden. I had bought a new lawnmower from Lidl the previous week and now was my chance to test drive it. The garden looked like a jungle, as we had not touched it since we had moved in the previous Autumn. Together we all assembled the bright orange lawnmower and plugged it into the extension lead running through the Dance Centre. As I mowed the lawn, the girls collected all the weeds and swept the patio and then we all sat down at our large wooden garden table for a delicious sandwich lunch. As I picked up my sandwich, the girls jumped up with joy and peeped through the holes in our reddish - brown garden fence. "Mummy, there here!" shouted Summer. I dropped my uneaten sandwich onto my plate and we all ran outside to meet them. David opened the car boot and I am not kidding you, they had brought everything with them, apart from the kitchen sink and their lively dog Mole. As the girls ran backwards and forwards up and down the stairs carrying bag after bag, suitcase after suitcase and pillow after pillow. I felt completely exhausted already and these were only our first visitors of the Summer. It was good to catch up with my sister again after such a long time and for her to spend time with the girls. Our next visitor was my friend, Vanessa Gardener who had travelled to Devon by train and Summer and I went to meet her at Torre station. We had seen Vanessa recently at Cecchetti Day in London. On Vanessa's visit she thoroughly spoiled us all with lovely gifts, a take away fish and chip dinner and on the following day before she left she took us all out for tea on the Babbacombe downs. It felt good to be spoiled and a treat for us all. The day after Vanessa left, our dear Nan Wen arrived and took us all out for dinner at a lovely pub called the Babbacombe Inn. What a delicious meal we all had. It was a lovely warm Summer's evening and I bought us all a variety of sweets to share with each other. There was salted caramel cheesecake, delicious sticky toffee pudding with vanilla ice cream and a warm chocolate brownie covered in lashings of fresh cream.

It was lovely having our family and friends to stay with us at our new home in Devon, it did feel very strange though, as we had not had family or friends to stay with us since 2019. The Summer term ended at the dance school and we were all very excited to start packing our suitcases in preparation for our Summer holiday to Corfu. I had booked a taxi to take us all to Bristol Airport and on Sunday 10th July 2022 we flew out to Corfu.

We arrived at Corfu Airport at midday, it was stiflingly hot and not a taxi insight. We walked along the back streets of Corfu Town lugging out suitcases behind us, stopping every couple of minutes gasping for a drink of water. Finally we made it to the blue bus station in San Rocco square, only to find out that we had just missed the number eleven bus to Pelekas and the next one was not due for another two hours. It was Sunday and everything was closed in Corfu Town, luckily I spotted a small cake shop and brought a large bowl of ice creams and a bottle of cold water for us all to share. We sat on the dusty stone wall under the olive tree in the buzzing San Rocco square, waiting for the number eleven bus to Pelekas. Finally we boarded our bus and arrived at our home in Pelekas, hot, exhausted and tired, having left Devon at 2am that morning. We made our beds and collapsed on top of them, we had arrived in paradise, our very special place. The hot sun was streaming through the gaps in the old wooden shutters as I woke up the next morning. I pulled myself out of bed and reached for a glass of cool water, the sound of buzzing was all around me. I went outside and pulled up an old rickety chair and plonked myself under a small tree in our courtyard. Above my head I could hear the piercing high-pitched buzzing sound, coming from the Cicada above me in the tree. The shrill sound of the hot summer days in Corfu was all around me, long gone were my days in England and teaching at Devon Dance Centre. For the next two months we would have no time, no day, we would not even know the date or what was going on in the world around us, unless of course I decided to connect to the internet or look at my mobile phone. This summer, I was going to write my autobiography, an enjoyable challenge for myself and a special gift for my three amazing daughters Shannon, Hafsa and Summer. Shannon was studying for her GCSE'S and Hafsa and Summer wanted to collect stones from the sea which they painted beautifully and sold to the many visiting tourists from all over the world that pass through our village during the summer months. When you stay in Pelekas you do not have to travel anywhere, if you are patient enough the world will come to you. Sitting on my balcony looking out to sea, I reflected back on my life and Little did I Know this is how it was going to turn out to be.

Spending time with Heather and Richard Glasstone

Me and my Girls

Printed in Great Britain
by Amazon